S0-BFG-489

Behind Practiced Smiles

HOLLYWOOD
ENTREPRENEUR

PETER MARIN

COPYRIGHT

Cover photo is Peter Marin with Luciano Pavarotti and Peter's co-producer Bobby Roberts after Pavarotti's incredible concert April 6, 2001, at the Indian Wells Tennis Gardens. The concert was sponsored by The City of Indian Wells and The Desert Sun, and was one of the most gratifying events of my career.

© Copyright ©2019 Peter Marin

All Rights Reserved

Cover Photo by Rand Larson Morningstar Productions, Palm Desert, Ca. Used by permission. All other photos courtesy of Marin Music.

ISBN: 9781796675849

DEDICATION

For Kim

ACKNOWLEDGEMENTS

I'd like to thank my dear friend and mentor, Richard Blue, who originally encouraged me to write this book. Richard's wisdom and continued gentle guidance are a gift.

Also, thank you to my patient and talented editor, Laurie Gibson, who has polished and polished this to a shine.

To my dear pal, Jack Millman, who called every day to ask that I read the newest pages to him. Now that's a pal!

And, of course, to my loving Kim, who on so many early mornings would quietly come into the room as I was writing, finding me often times sobbing recalling old memories, and softly hug me from behind and tell me that it was worth it; she was right.

Thank you!

CONTENTS

Chapter I

CATCHING MY DREAM

It seems I was destined to be in and around show business. As a young child, maybe three or four years old, my father brought home his friend Jimmie Rodgers. At the time, Jimmie Rodgers was as big as Elvis Presley. He had hit records and TV shows, and his concerts were sellouts. He was a huge star. Jimmie and his wife and their frisky white toy poodle would come to our home in San Pedro, California, to have dinner with my parents. Those dinners would take place under a blanket of secrecy. My sister, Michele, and I would have to promise never to tell that the Rodgers were coming to town. If the neighbors knew, my parents feared pandemonium would break out. Although my sister and I were too young to fully appreciate this, we kept our traps shut. To Michele and me, they were just Mr. and Mrs. Rodgers, whom we liked very much. When they would visit, after dinner, Jimmie would get out his guitar. I clearly remember being put on Jimmie's knee as he would sing and play his guitar and laugh and have such a great time entertaining our family. Although my father was an aspiring actor, we really were not a show business family.

We were just a regular, small-town group, which is why I think Jimmie enjoyed it so much. Later, when I was in my late teens and early twenties, Jimmie was very helpful to me in my singing career. He had a studio in Hollywood where he would edit his music and films,

PROMO SHOT OF ME AT APPROXIMATELY 20 YEARS OF AGE

mostly children's films that he was doing at that time, and we would meet there. Although he was very busy with his productions, he never seemed too busy to see me. He was always happy to advise me however he could. Quite a few times, I recall, he brought up fondly those dinners in San Pedro with my family when I was a small child. What a kind and generous man Jimmie is. I stayed in touch with Jimmie on and off for many, many years.

Once when I was twenty-one, I was in Reno, Nevada, sitting in the lounge where he was performing. He sang the song "Honeycomb," one of his many hits, after which he asked the audience, "Do you remember where you were when you first heard laughs and smiles from Jimmie, I called out, "I was sitting on your lap!" He immediately put his hand up to shield his eyes from the spotlight and looked out to scan the audience and said, "Petey, is that you?" I called out, "Sure is, Jimmie," and we ended up spending that entire evening together, til 7am when, after breakfast, we parted ways. That was a great night with a wonderful man and entertainer. But, I think I'm getting ahead of myself. Jimmie was just the start of my introduction to show business.

I mentioned earlier that my father was an actor. Well, that may be overstating it. He was a lot of things. He was a restaurateur and, for thirty years, a chief steward for American President Lines, the cruise ships that toured the world. And, yes, he was a bit-part actor. But acting was really the least of it. He dreamed of being an actor and although he did get small parts in many television shows, such as Bonanza, Police Woman, The New Breed, etc., he really didn't find a career in acting. But through his position with American President Lines, being essentially the maître d' on high-end cruise ships, he made friends with the rich and famous.

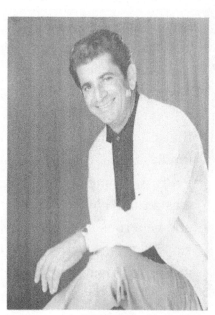

PETE MARINO

My dad was good looking and witty, classy, funny, and

3

somewhat of a rogue, which added to his charm. As a young boy watching him on television for ten or fifteen seconds at a time, I'm sure that added to my desire to be in showbusiness. I also remember, although I could not have been more than four years old, being on the floor in my pajamas (you know the kind, with the feet in them), sitting cross-legged, leaning against my mother's legs as we watched Andy Williams singing on television. I looked up at her and said, "Mom, that's what I want to do. I want to be a singer." I remember that moment today as if it happened yesterday, clear as a bell. I don't remember my mother's response, but I'm sure she'd rather I was hoping to be a doctor or a lawyer or something other than an artist.

My mother was a fabulous pianist, as was her mother before her. She became a pianist by default, however. Her first instrument was cello, which she was so good at that by age twelve she sat second chair in the Long Beach Philharmonic Orchestra. She said she became self-conscious straddling the instrument, so she switched to piano. Truly a musical genius, by age seventeen she was so good that the Walt Disney Company offered her a job in their music department. But she turned it down to marry my dad, a decision, except for having my sister and me, I think she secretly regrets. So, you see, between my mom, the musician, and my dad, the frustrated actor, I was somewhat destined for a life in the arts.

I was put in Catholic school, Holy Trinity, in San Pedro. Except for a steady streak of disciplinary issues, I really don't have any specific memories other than falling head over heels for a cute kindergarten girl named Nannette when I was in first grade. That lasted until fifth grade when she moved to San Diego. Really broke me up, her moving away... I don't think I'd won a game of two square in the four years I was courting her. The only other highlight of my young school years was being called out of the school choir when I was eleven to sing for a parishioner's daughter's wedding. I was paid $20 cash to sing one song and boy, was I hooked. My singing career had begun. Twenty dollars!

My mother had tried to interest me in playing an instrument, but I could never sit still long enough to get through a lesson, let alone practice. I took piano lessons, guitar lessons, violin lessons, even bongo lessons! I'd get these itching attacks like I was allergic to music lessons! Oh, my poor mother. But when that gentleman handed me a twenty-dollar bill for singing a song, I was home, baby! Like I'd said as a toddler, that's what I wanted to do.

Within a year or so I formed a garage band and started playing private parties and local junior high dances. We were playing the current rock songs of the day, R&B, Motown, things like that. Dance tunes, and, as I recall, we weren't half bad. Things took a real turn for me though when I was fifteen. I tried out a new drummer, a younger kid—he was thirteen! Ha! A kid named Johnny Profeta. I had been told that even though he was younger, he was a good drummer and, just as important, he had a rehearsal spot. He had a basement at his house and his parents would let us practice there.

At our first rehearsal I noticed a man come down and sit on the steps. He was very attentive and seemed interested in what I was doing. I figured it was Johnny's dad. When rehearsal was over this man introduced himself to me as Johnny's dad, Johnny Prophet. He brought me upstairs and sat me down with him at a white grand piano in their living room, which, as it turned out, was a gift from Liberace. He told me that he was a professional singer, and that he thought I had a great voice for jazz, but not so much for rock 'n' roll and R&B. He said he'd liked to coach me and teach me how to become not just a singer but an entertainer. He thought I had what it took. He then showed me his albums he had recorded for Reprieve Records, Frank Sinatra's record label.

As we sat at the piano, he asked me if I knew certain songs, songs from the Great American Songbook. Standards, most of which I knew because my mother was always playing those songs on the record player or the piano. Because of her, there was always great music in the house: Tony Bennett, Frank Sinatra, Keely Smith. So, when Johnny asked me if I knew the songs, I was at least familiar with them. We started working together right away. I'd come over to his house in the afternoon and we'd work on songs. He'd explain the meaning of the lyric, how I should convey it vocally, how I should present myself physically, what I should be doing with my body, when to smile, when to laugh, hell—even how to laugh! He taught me everything he could. Johnny was a great entertainer and a great singer.

At the time he was billed as the highest-paid lounge singer in the business. He was a sought-after studio singer because he could sight-read music like nobody's business. He packed every nightclub that he worked. The consummate professional. I was so fortunate to have caught his attention. So, after a few months of coaching at his house, he invited me to be a guest on his show. He was working at a club called the Delray in Fullerton, California. Still being fifteen, I didn't have a driver's license and my mother was not keen on my singing in nightclubs, so I kinda snuck out one Friday night. I talked an older girl from school into driving me. She was a singer too, a senior at school at the time and we drove out there... It must have been a forty-minute drive and I'll never forget, I sang "Summertime," and baby, I was scared to death. But once I had two or three words out of my mouth, I started to relax and just do what I was taught and sing and act as Johnny showed me.

When I was done, the crowd erupted in applause and this fifteen-year-old brought the house down! Well, that did it for me. I knew then and there that I wanted to be a nightclub performer. What a feeling. Standing next to the piano and drums, looking out at those people, smiling and clapping for me. Wow, that was it, man—that was it! Johnny, in his beautiful suit, rushed up and took the mic from my hand and said, "Ladies and gentlemen, Pete Marino, my protégé!" Wow, was I ever proud, and so was he. We continued for a short while after that, still meeting at his house weekly, going over songs, improving my repertoire, talking about music theory, and generally what it means to be a professional. And, he continued to invite me to be a guest on his show.

What started out as that one song gradually grew to my doing a full forty minutes? I was somewhat of a novelty being a long-haired, hippie-looking kid singing these jazz standards. Being underage, you know, and not even having a driver's license, I had to find someone to drive me out there, and again, I'd sneak out because Mom didn't want me to go... Funny thing, the owners of the place, the Smith Brothers, would always pay me with a case of Lancer's wine. They would put it in the trunk of the car that brought me that night. Lancer's was the wine in the little brown bottles—that's how I got paid! Oh, those were the days! Then one night, I thought I'd be really cute and do a little bit right when I started my part of the show. Johnny introduced me, and I came up and took the microphone from him. He left the stage and sat down at a table with three women.

I took a piece of paper from my pocket and said, "Hey, Johnny, I stopped by your house on my way to the club and your wife gave me this note to read to you..." And I started singing "Please Release Me," which was a big Engel Bert Humperdinck hit, and the crowd roared with laughter! Johnny was laughing and shaking his finger at me, jokingly, I thought. But after my set, he took me out to the parking lot and gave me the riot act! He said, "Don't EVER mention my wife, EVER! You see all those women in there? Half of them are hoping to fuck me, and the other half I've already fucked! They don't know I'm married! You see a ring? No. 'Cause I don't wear one! This is my business: the women come to see me, the men come to pick them up—that's how it works! God damn it, kid! Now get the fuck outta here!" I was crushed. I thought I was being clever and entertaining... I had no idea! My idol had just torn me a new one, and to be honest, I really didn't get it. I had no clue that he was fooling around. When we were at his house, everything seemed fine. He, as it turned out, just had a thing for the ladies. Needless to say, things cooled between us. While this was going on most weekends, I was also singing at high school parties and dances, doing some weddings on the side, hustling up any music gigs I could. I've got to backtrack a bit here, because there are paths that will intertwine in my story. Besides music, as a young boy I also enjoyed playing baseball. I was quite good. I was a skinny kid, quick on my feet. I was always an all-star second baseman: peewee league, little league, all the way through pony league. I mention this because it was in little league that I met Andy Martinez. Andy was six or seven years my senior and in spite of that, we became best friends. We also shared a passion for golf. Andy and I would practice golf nearly every day after school or weekends. Whenever we could, we played at Rolling Hills Country Club, where we were allowed basically to play for free, or damn near. At this point my mother was a single parent and Andy, although his parents were married, was from a large but poor family, yet somehow, we were able to play golf at the country club, mostly I think because of the kindness of the club pro, Pat Chartrand.

By the time I was twelve and Andy was eighteen, we were pretty good players. I was never as good as Andy, but I could hold my own. When Andy turned eighteen, he won the men's championship. As a reward our club pro Pat asked Andy to caddy for him at a Monday qualifying round for a PGA tournament, The Haig Scotch Foursome, which was held in Orange County.

I went along, too. I had no idea really what caddying was all about, but I got the day off of school to go along and to see if I could "pick up a bag." As it turned out, I got hired to caddy by a brand-new pro who was playing in his first tournament. He had just qualified for his tour card, so he was almost as green as me! Now I must add that although I was only thirteen, I carried myself as if I were a bit older and, being a good Italian boy, had a healthy bit of facial hair already. I easily could pass for eighteen, so I got hired in the parking lot by Grier Jones. Pat and Andy headed out to attempt to qualify.

Grier and I went to the range and practiced until the qualifiers cleared out, and then we played a practice round. Afterward, Grier and I walked to his car, so I could put his clubs in his trunk, and up walked Pat and Andy. Introductions all around, at which point Grier said, "Okay, Pete, see you tomorrow morning at 6:30."

"What do you mean? I've got to go back to school tomorrow," I told him, not realizing that I'd been hired for the entire week! Fortunately, Pat didn't qualify, so I suggested that Andy caddy for Grier. Andy worked for Grier Jones on the tour for a couple of years until he was hired by Johnny Miller. Andy Martinez went on to have a wonderful career as one of the most successful and respected professional caddies. He worked for Johnny Miller maybe fifteen years, certainly through Johnny's heyday. It was through Andy that I started caddying PGA tournaments.

My first one was the L.A. Open. It seemed as if the air was charged with electricity. Everywhere I looked there was excitement and more famous golfers than I'd ever seen in one place. That week I caddied for Art Wall, a former Masters winner. He was a quiet gentleman who wanted nothing more of me than to carry and clean his clubs and tend the pin. Easy, thank God, 'cause truth be known, I was pretty overwhelmed. By Wednesday, when the Pro-Am took place, I had settled down and wasn't so star struck. I remember that Pro-Am. It was my fourteenth birthday, and Jan Murray, the comedian, was the celebrity in our group. He caught wind that it was my birthday and took every opportunity to tease me about it. Crazy—here I was, just a kid, really, working with a Masters winner and getting ribbed by a famous comedian... wow! Anyway, after the round, I searched everywhere for Andy Martinez, who was going to give me a ride home.

Most everyone had left by then.

There were a few pros and celebrities hanging out in the restaurant, but, being a caddy, I wasn't allowed in there. All the spectators had gone, and as I checked the near-empty parking lot, I was getting panicked. It was getting dark and I was cold and anxious because my whole family—my mom, sister, aunts, uncles, cousins— were all going to be at our house for my birthday dinner. And Andy had left without me! Just then, Jan Murray and Joey Bishop pulled up in Mr. Bishop's SL Mercedes Benz and stopped next to me. Jan asked me what I was doing, so I told him I thought I'd missed my ride. He introduced me to Joey Bishop and told Joey it was my birthday. He immediately offered to take me home, even after I explained that I lived an hour's drive away in San Pedro.

Mr. Bishop dropped the convertible top and I squeezed into the small space behind the passenger seats and we started out of the parking lot. All I could think of was the look on the faces of my family when I'd walk in the house with Jan Murray and Joey Bishop! These two guys were huge stars, and my Uncle Tony loved Joey Bishop! That was gonna top it all! But wouldn't you just know it, as we hit the driveway, in came Andy, yelling his apologies!

Because of Andy, I could always caddy any PGA tournament I wanted to. I'd let him know which one, and he'd line up a "bag" for me with a pro. Since I was still in school and busy with singing on weekends, I'd only caddy Southern California tournaments. Let's just say I was a "fair weather" caddy. I had no interest in going to the Bing Crosby Clambake in Monterey, where the weather was miserable! So, until I got out of high school, I stuck to the L.A. Open, The Bob Hope (in Palm Springs), The Andy Williams (in San Diego), and a few satellite Southern California events. I had a ball caddying! To spend the day working in groups with greats like Arnold Palmer, Jack Nicklaus, Gary Player, Lee Trevino, and Johnny Miller, to name just a few, was a dream come true. All the players were nice to us caddies, and I remember always being treated very well.

Between caddies and players, there was a family atmosphere. Although I wasn't full time, most of the guys traveled year-round and worked for the same pro week after week, so it was like an extended family. The caddies I hung around with were Andy's friends, a great bunch of twenty-something hippies who, even though I was a few years younger, took me right in. The work week started Monday morning if your pro had to qualify, or Monday afternoon or Tuesday early morning to walk the course to get the yardage. Walking the course was fun but serious work. We would often do this in groups, as everyone had to get it done pretty much at the same time. In those days, we'd have a small notebook where we'd draw a diagram of each hole and green, marking where certain things were, like a stream, or tree, or valley, and sprinkler heads. We'd use the sprinkler heads as reference points from which to walk the yardage off to the front, middle, and back of the green, which of course, we also measured.

With today's radar systems, you're probably thinking that our measuring system using our feet was fairly inaccurate, but it wasn't. We would practice our paces at one-yard intervals, over and over, so that muscle memory took over and accuracy was constant. Earlier I mentioned that we would get the yardages in groups. Oftentimes, we would check each other. No one wanted another caddy to have bad yardages. We really were like family and looked out for each other. I remember one Tuesday for a practice round at the Colonial in Fort Worth, Texas, my friend Pete Bender was sick and asked if I could cover for him that afternoon. He was caddying for Lanny Wadkins. Of course, I helped out. All was going well until on one hole late in the round Lanny asked me for the yardage to the middle of the green, and I checked my notes and said, "A hundred fifteen yards." He pulled a club from the bag, got set, and swung—and no sooner finished his swing when he said, "Let's check your yardage, pard, 'cause I hit that 115, and it's long!" And it was, by four yards. My step was off! Just enough to cost a pro a tournament! By the way, Lanny hit that ball 117 yards according to our count when we walked it. He wasn't mad. He just wanted to make sure that he was right and that I had it right, because that's the attitude that prevailed.

It was really a nice environment, and a great way for a kid to see the best golfers in the world behaving like some of the best people in the world. After you had the yardages marked, you'd meet up with your pro at the range. In those days, we'd drop a bunch of balls and head out to catch them. That's right, he'd hit the ball at you as you stood out in the range. As he'd change clubs, he'd wave you back... and back...

and back until he was hitting driver. Dangerous duty. Once you survived that, you'd get a breather while your pro practiced putting. Then it was out to the course. Wednesday was Pro-Am Day, usually fun, but a lot of work. As the pro caddy, all the amateur players rely on you for advice, mostly reading putts. There was a circus atmosphere on Wednesday, too, because of all the celebrities. This set a magical mood, and more good news was that they all tipped the pro caddy, so it could be a good day at the office as well.

Thursday morning at first light, all the caddies were out getting pin placements. You had to visit all eighteen greens and measure how many paces from the front, side and back, right or left, the pin was placed. We were not allowed on the greens, so this could take some time. Good thing we were young and in good shape because we were running our asses off! We had to be done before the first tee times, and they went off sometimes as early as 7:30! This ritual repeated Friday morning at sunrise regardless of your tee time, and on good weeks, if you made the cut, on Saturday and Sunday morning, too. Some days could be pretty long.

And although the days might have been long, they were never boring. I always had a sense of awe that I was surrounded the world's best golfers, and on Pro-Am days, by some of the biggest names in show business—and many of these great athletes and stars called me by name! I was at golf courses that were so beautiful that calendars were made about them. I was one lucky kid.

But golf wasn't my first love, singing was, and my caddy buddies knew it. I think it was Pete Bender who nicknamed me "The Singing Caddy!" By now, Andy Martinez had been working for Johnny Miller for a while, who, if you don't know, was the Tiger Woods of that time. Johnny was dominating the tour, and Andy, with his long black hair and his handsome Aztec Indian features, was becoming almost as famous! Well, Andy, through his partnership with Johnny, got to know many celebrities. So, he thought it might be helpful to me if he hooked me up with Andy Williams as his caddy for the Pro-Ams. Andy told Mr. Williams about me, "The Singing Caddy," and he hired me right away. The first week I worked for Andy Williams was at The Bob Hope Desert Classic, in Palm Springs.

That was an unusual tournament in that the Pro-Am section was four days, Wednesday through Saturday, instead for just one, on Wednesday. Andy had me come down early, on Monday. He wanted to practice on Monday and Tuesday, so I met him at his home at La Quinta Country Club. I remember him greeting me warmly and saying something like, "So you're the singing caddy, eh?" He instructed me to meet him at the clubhouse, where we met shortly after. I was waiting by the practice green when he came up with another man that he introduced as his producer, Pierre Cossette. He introduced me as Pete, The Singing Caddy, to which Mr. Cossette made some smart-ass remark like, "That sounds like a dead-end career." I don't need to tell you we never got along. He was a loud-mouth, pompous ass who thought he was God's gift to everything and everyone. I ended up carrying doubles that day, meaning, I caddied for both of them. What a pain in the rear. They hit it all over the place. Andy hit it left, Pierre was in the right rough and vice versa all day long—in the hot desert sun! Andy, as I recall, was being overly nice that day, probably to make up for Pierre being such an ass. Man, what a long day! Fortunately, Andy said that Pierre couldn't join us Tuesday!

Anyway, as memory serves, the next day was kind of fun. It was just Andy and me. He asked me about my singing. I told him about the kind of work I was doing and when I told him that I had been tutored by

14

Johnny Prophet, he was really impressed! He knew Johnny very well and told me a few stories that were more than enlightening! According to Andy, Johnny had a promising career, but he had crossed Sinatra. Seems Johnny was messing around with one of Sinatra's girlfriends on the sly and got caught! According to the tale, Sinatra had Johnny blacklisted in all of the casinos in Nevada and Atlantic City, effectively putting the kibosh on his career. Seems like Johnny's need to chase the girls cost him a lot. Anyway, Andy and I had found some common ground and it looked like we were going to get along just fine. We even sang a few songs together that day, and he told me that he thought I sounded great! Imagine that! Humming along, singing with Andy Williams—the guy who had made me want to be a singer to begin with!

The Bob Hope Desert Classic wasn't like the other PGA tournaments, maybe with the exception of the Bing Crosby Clambake, in that it attracted the biggest celebrities in sports, politics, and show business, and kept them in town all week. It was one big party! Bob Hope set the tone, which meant the first order of business was to have a good time. Of course, the pros were there to make a living, but they couldn't help getting caught up the magical, almost circus-like atmosphere that permeated the grounds. Movie stars and TV stars mingled with recording artists and heads of state, playing (usually) bad golf, laughing it off while signing autographs by day and partying by night. It was a time and place like no other, and the crowds loved having such intimate access to these luminaries. For me, it was even more magical.

Although I had worked PGA tournaments before, and had gotten to know some big-name pros, and, through my singing and caddying, had met many celebrities. But working with Andy Williams at the Bob Hope put me in a whole new position. And because Andy was somewhat taken with me as "The Singing Caddy" and kind of impressed with my background and abilities, he right away sort of adopted me. He said he wanted to help me and started to introduce me to his friends: "This is Pete Marino, The Singing Caddy. You should hear this kid sing! Do you remember Johnny Prophet? Johnny discovered him!" That's the way he'd introduce me... to the biggest stars you could imagine! This started about 7:30 on that first Wednesday morning of the Hope! I met Dinah Shore, Bob Hope, so many stars, all before we teed off!

But one of the biggest moments of my life happened that morning when Frank Sinatra walked up, and Andy introduced me as Pete Marino, The Singing Caddy. Mr. Sinatra shook my hand and said, "Nice to meet you—are you Petey's kid?" Now, I must tell you, at this point, I hadn't had contact with my father for about ten years, and although I wasn't surprised that he knew Mr. Sinatra, I was pretty shocked by this whole conversation. Frank Sinatra was, to me, the biggest and brightest star in the universe, and here I was, with my hand in his, having a little chat about my dad, the rogue! Well, not letting on that my father and I weren't all that close, I replied that, yes, I was Petey's kid. "You look just like him," Mr. Sinatra said as he gave my cheek a friendly double slap. "Tell him hello for me, will ya? Nice meeting ya, Kid." Then he and Andy exchanged some words that may just have well have taken place miles away.

I'd just met Frank Sinatra. No, I'd just had a conversation with the Chairman of the Board! For someone who thought that he was beyond being able to be star struck, I was as stricken as one could imagine. I didn't know it then, but that would be the start of a long, friendly acquaintance with Mr. Sinatra.

Andy Williams, that first week at the Bob Hope Desert Classic, treated me great! He introduced me to his friends and family, spoke to me kindly, and offered to help me with my singing career. Our amateur group won first place that week, and Andy even gave me credit for aiding in that! He said that we were a great team, and he looked forward to working with me both on and off the golf course. The next week, I was caddying for him at his tournament in San Diego—La Jolla, to be exact —The Andy Williams San Diego Open at Torrey Pines Golf Club. As the tournament's host, he was putting on a show for the sponsors and the celebrities at the Town and Country Hotel in San Diego on that Wednesday night. This show would feature big stars, and Andy thought that it would be good experience and exposure for me to do a song. I was so excited! I was going on right after Buddy Hackett.

I remember on that Monday morning Andy and I were talking to Buddy at the golf course about the show. Andy told Buddy that I'd be going on right after him, and, because I was so young, and that it was a family show, to please keep his act clean, to which Buddy replied, "Oh, Andy, I'd never fuck up your show"! Being completely caught off-guard, Andy and I doubled over in laughter.

Man, I could hardly control my excitement. Being on an Andy Williams show, even though this was a small, private event, and following Buddy Hackett was so much bigger than anything I'd ever done, but it was something I felt ready for. I was pumped!

To sweeten the pot, Miss World, USA was also on the show. Lynda Carter, who went on to have the hit TV series Wonder Woman, had just been crowned Miss World, USA. Because it was Andy's tournament, Lynda joined our group and walked with us inside the ropes during the Pro-Am round. That didn't go so well; for Andy, it was lust at first sight! He couldn't tear himself away from her for an instant! It was embarrassing! He was hitting on her so hard that after an hour or so, she started hanging around me, for protection, I think. This did not set too well with Mr. Williams. Although Lynda tried to be casual with all of this, it was obvious that she was uncomfortable. Her seeking asylum with me only made me uncomfortable, because that put me smack dab in the middle! At one point, Andy pulled me aside and told me to stop hanging around with her, 'cause she needed to be with him, the star, not me, the caddy, and I should tell her so!

Well, here we go. Seemed his attitude towards me was starting to change.

I remember that Lynda was a really sweet girl. She joked about Andy being old enough to be her father, and that she was glad that we were on a golf course because she'd hate to think what he'd try if they were alone. She, too, was looking forward to being on the show that night, as singing was her real talent, even though it was her stunning good looks that won her worldwide recognition. She thought them calling me "The Singing Caddy" was pretty funny, as I recall, and she was really happy for me that I was also on the show. It really was kind of a big deal. Anyway, she roughed it out for a while and rejoined Andy. He just couldn't control himself! He kept putting his arm around her, pulling her to him, which looked pretty funny because she towered over him. After another hour or so, she wandered back my way, walking up the fairway with me for a hole, complaining that he was becoming quite suggestive. She seemed genuinely uncomfortable, but when Andy called, she had little choice but to rejoin him. At the next tee box, Andy called me aside, and angrily under his breath told me that I was off the show that night because I didn't listen to him about staying away from Lynda Carter. I was stunned. I don't think I said a word. We finished the round, Andy paid me, and I walked to my car, still stunned.

I saw the other side of Andy Williams. In just a week and a half, he had gone from full supporter to a mean-spirited, cold elitist. In just a few hours, I went from being treated as "The Singing Caddy" to the lowly caddy. His taking me off that show really hurt me. That show represented his trust and belief in my talent and his willingness to attest to it. His taking me off the show destroyed all of that and left me really down. I saw Andy many times throughout that week, as I stayed in town to see the tournament. He hardy acknowledged me, and I really didn't know how to act. A week or so later, he called me because he wanted me to caddy for him down in the desert, at Dinah Shore's event, I think. He acted like nothing ever happened. I'm not proud of it, but I took the job. In spite of everything, he paid me a lot of money. He was nice again, getting me to sing with him while we were on the course. He started giving me tips on breathing and phrasing whenever we were alone. He'd introduce me as his protégé, from time to time, and being young and naive, I was hanging on to the hope that he'd actually help me. This went on off and on for a couple of years; he'd call, and I'd work for him.

The L.A. Open; The Bob Hope, his tournament in San Diego, and a few random days or weeks here and there. His "mentoring" was helpful but his promises to advance my career were always empty. If Andy needed you, he treated you like a prince, if he didn't, he treated you like crap. Although his image was all Mom and apple pie, he was anything but! Our relationship ended where it began, at La Quinta Country Club, and with whom it began, Pierre Cossette. It was my last day working for them. After the round, they knew I was anxious to get back to Los Angeles, San Pedro, actually.

Not being able to go inside (no caddies allowed), after fifteen minutes or so I started waving at Andy to get his attention. Just then, a couple of ladies joined them, as he gave me a signal to hold on for a minute or two. Another ten minutes, I waved, he signaled... more time goes by and I waved...another signal... Finally, I asked the valet to please bring Mr. Williams' Rolls-Royce convertible around, which he happily did. I opened the trunk and put Andy and Pierre's clubs in. Then I got in the car, put down the top, and waved at them as they looked at me in shock as I slowly—very slowly—drove away.

You've never seen anything so funny as these two running after me, yelling and calling me everything under the sun! I finally drove back around the circular drive and before turning over the keys, demanded my pay. Andy counted out hundred-dollar bills, as was his customary way of paying me, and I tossed him the keys and got out of the Rolls. At this point, Pierre started to laugh hysterically, but Andy wasn't too happy. I guess I'd finally had enough of his B.S. Andy was in so many ways everything that I wanted to be, yet, the way he treated me and others deeply disappointed me. Andy Williams, I was learning, just like the rest of us, was no angel, even though he had the smile and the voice of one. Our paths would cross again.

AT PGA WEST WITH GOLFING LEGEND TOM LEHMAN AND MY LIFELONG PAL ANDY MARTINEZ

Chapter 2

MAKING MY WAY

I met Andy Williams when I was seventeen. Throughout this time, when I wasn't in school, I stayed busy with my bands, working private parties and the occasional wedding gigs, as well as some part-time jobs, anything to keep afloat. When I was eighteen, I did my first four-hour nightclub gig where I was the headliner. It was in my hometown of San Pedro, at the Tasman Sea Restaurant. The Tasman Sea was an upscale restaurant with a piano bar area, a dance floor behind which were dark maroon leather booths spread out in a half circle. Very chic, especially for a fishing and harbor town. Adjacent to the restaurant was a motel, so I'm sure you get the picture. Unbeknownst to this wet-behind-the-ears kid, it was a pick-up joint for middle-aged divorcees.

And here I thought I had packed the place just on my good name alone! Well, I did have all my friends show up, even my high school drama teacher. The night, divorcees and all, was a huge success! My career was off to a fine start, or so I thought. Reality set in quickly, as it turned out that it was hard to find work for a jazz-singing, long-haired, hippy-looking kid; everybody wanted rock bands and dance bands.

Good thing I still had my bands playing that kind of music, but I really didn't like it, and I felt like a fish out of water performing it. I was a jazz singer, and rock just didn't resonate with me. So, I kept plugging and looking for venues that would feature me and my type of music. Finally, a very nice place in north Long Beach called the Winchester Inn hired me. It seems they had heard of me from the owners of the Tasman Sea, and said they'd take a chance with me. All excited, my trio and I arrived to set up about 5:00 on a Saturday evening, and as the guys were setting up, the owner asked me what instrument I played. I told him that I was the singer. He was a huge Italian guy, 350 pounds at least, and he looked at all 125 pounds of me and said, "I don't pay nobody's just ta sing, so what daya play?" Again, I told him I was the singer. So, he said, "I'm not payin' yous a dime, not just ta sing, who da ya think ya is, Sinatra? I'll take twenty-five percent off the agreement, and the guys can play." My guys heard this, and without saying a word, started packing up their gear and we were out of there. We heard about it, though. I can only imagine what he called us, as every word was in Italian.

I sure was proud of my guys, though. I know they could have used the money. We were all a bunch of busted-out kids, but, hey, you gotta draw the line somewhere. Loyalty. It was about this time that I heard of an artist manager in Hollywood by the name of Paul Henderson.

Word was that Mr. Henderson was well connected with the good clubs in town and the record executives at the major companies, but he was exceptionally picky about the acts he'd represent. I started calling him and after a few weeks was able to arrange an audition. One of the acts that he represented was Don Cunningham, who, along with his wife had a great show band that was huge in Japan. The band happened to be stateside for a couple of months and, Mr. Henderson had them booked at a swanky hotel in Hollywood, which is where I was invited to sit in. I don't recall the name of the hotel, but I do remember that it was quite upscale.

I arrived with my dear friend and musical director, Brian Asher. Brian had been playing electric bass with me since I was thirteen. He was, rest his beautiful soul, a true musical genius and a beautiful person. Brian came from a musical family. His father played French horn; his mother, harpsichord and piano; his sister, violin; and Brian, the cello, as well as electric bass. He was a couple of years older than me, and when we met, we immediately became as close as brothers. His family would perform classical concerts, and I would be his mother's page turner. We were nearly inseparable into my early twenties. Anyway, Brian and I met Mr. Henderson and joined him at his table as we watched Don Cunningham and Company, as they were known, tear it up! Man were they great! I remember getting pretty nervous waiting to go on—having to follow Don's thoroughly polished and professional show—thinking how important this audition was.

The pressure was mounting and Brian, who really was a seasoned performer, sensed this. He leaned over to me and whispered some stupid, silly joke that was his style, and completely relaxed me.

Soon after that, Don Cunningham introduced me, and I joined him on stage and sang "Summertime," the George Gershwin classic, which, incidentally, was the first song I ever sang when I was Johnny Prophet's guest. Thanks to Brian's silly joke, I was nice and relaxed, and the audition went wonderfully. The next day, I drove to the Hollywood Hills to Paul Henderson's house and I officially had a manager. Nineteen years old and I had a real, honest-to-goodness manager!

Paul was the quintessential manager, straight out of central casting! Although he was only in his early forties, he was recently retired and had moved to the West Coast from Manhattan. He had had a seat on the New York Stock Exchange and had been quite successful. He was also recently divorced from a TV news reporter, and had sole custody of his two sons, a pretty unusual thing, especially in those days. Well, Paul was anything but usual. Although he kind of fit the stereotype of a fast-talking New York pitchman, he had a heart of gold, and we truly came to love each other as family. One of the first gigs Paul booked me on was a small, dark club off the beaten path in West Hollywood. In those days, bookings were usually for a few nights a week, for a few weeks or even a few months in duration. In this case, as I remember, he got a call for someone to fill in last minute for a singer who got sick, and that fill-in someone was me.

My trio and I went in just for the night, but it was memorable because it was the second time I talked with Mr. Sinatra. It was a weeknight, maybe Wednesday or Thursday, and the place was pretty empty. It was also pretty dark. At some point, a few guys came in and sat at a back table. I really didn't pay much attention. As I was heading to the restroom on my break, someone called to me, "Hey, Petey, come over here." Now, my name, Pete Marino, along with my picture was up in the lobby (Paul always insisted on this), but nobody called me Petey; that was my dad's nickname. As I turned, I see Mr. Sinatra with a

24

couple of other guys, and he was waving me over! I shook his hand and he asked if I was still caddying. I can't believe he remembered me! He complimented me on my singing and asked about my father, and he was as kind and gracious as could be. I was stunned. It all lasted but a moment or two, and I carried on. I remembered as I approached the bandstand to begin the next set, Mr. S. waved as he and his pals left. Can you imagine, Frank Sinatra recognized me and remembered my name. Wow!!! The guys in the band were pretty impressed! Hell, I was pretty impressed!

Paul worked tirelessly on my behalf and kept me working on a pretty steady basis. Most of the gigs were in or around Los Angeles, Hollywood and Beverly Hills. Some went as far north as Santa Barbara, or even out to Palm Springs. One morning I got a call from Paul, he was excited! He woke me up, it must've been 6:30 in the morning and told me to pack because I was flying to Orlando on the red-eye that night! Turned out that a group that wanted Paul to manage them had a singer quit and they needed a replacement asap! They were under contract for two more months and had to fulfill the terms of it, so Paul, somehow dangling a carrot, got them to guarantee me a fat contract, play or not. So, I flew out that night, rehearsed the next morning, and got ready for that night's show.

It turned out that the drummer and the female singer were married and were the leaders of the band. My predecessor didn't quit, he got fired, because he and the wife were fooling around! Well, I couldn't even do my first show with this group because the husband and wife had a huge fight and split up on the spot! The good news is, they wrote me a check, as per the contract that Paul had them sign, for the entire two months! I was home in Los Angeles the following day with two months' pay, for one rehearsal (less Paul's percentage, of course!).

Soon after, Paul booked a gig for me north of L.A., in Westlake Village. Westlake Village is near Thousand Oaks, California, and these two towns were both upscale and becoming popular with people in the entertainment industry. Hollywood was a little less than an hour's drive, Malibu was right over some beautiful rolling hills, so access to everything in the business was close, with the feeling of being in the country. I was originally booked Wednesday through Saturday nights, for a couple of months, but that gig lasted more than two years.

At first the club was called "The Golden Rib," and was a high-brow dinner house. By the time I got there, it had been open for a few years, and did good business on the weekends. After a few months, I developed a pretty good following, but the dinner business was starting to slip. My father, whom I had reunited with when I was about eighteen or nineteen, lived in Thousand Oaks and was a regular at the club. He also became friends with the owner, and with his food and beverage background, became a consultant for the place. At that time, there was a craze for oyster bars, and my dad knew a guy who managed them very successfully (he called himself "Johnny Clams"!). Well, my dad, seeing as the dining business had died off, convinced the owner to change the direction of the restaurant, to hire my dad as the manager, bring in an oyster bar with Johnny Clams, and to change the name to "Captain Calamari" just as the oyster bar craze died! Worst timing ever! Within months, the only part of the place with any action was the bar, but even that wasn't enough to support my trio Wednesday through Saturday. It got to the point that each payday, the guys in the band would rush to the bank to cash their checks, because inevitably, at least one wouldn't clear! With my father managing the place, I became so embarrassed that I stopped taking my checks to the bank so that my bandmates' checks would clear. Soon after, I cut back to three nights a week, then let the drummer go...then the bass

player...then down to just performing on Friday and Saturday. I fel
horrible for my dad, and for my bandmates.

I talked to Paul and he started looking for another gig for me, which he
found at The Airport Park Marina Hotel, adjacent to The Forum, in
Inglewood. I had a six-week engagement, but there was a condition:
had to feature a female singer, and I had to play dance music. Well, it
was better than nothing (or so I thought), so I auditioned singers
hired a good one, added some dance tunes, and we went to work
Problem was, the singer I hired had a drinking problem and got
sloshed every night. After the second week, I gave her two weeks
notice. The next night on the gig, she brought her boyfriend, a guy
had never met. He was about 280 pounds of anger, and just so
happened to be the sergeant of arms of one of L.A.'s more notorious
biker gangs, The Chosen Few. For added effect, I suppose, he brought
along a bunch of his friends! He told me that they were there to get
her job back. I said something about not being able to do that.

She finished out her two weeks begrudgingly, and he, along with a
threatening group of bikers sitting at the front tables, would glare at
me all night. I think the presence of the L.A. Lakers basketball players
and fans being there served as a buffer, but I gotta tell you, that was a
long two weeks. Unbeknownst to everyone, after the first night I met
the bikers, I carried a .38 snub nose pistol in a holster under my
jacket, just in case, and hotel security walked me to and from my car
every night.

With that experience, I was pretty down on things, and to make
matters worse, Paul was having trouble finding me a gig that wasn't
another dance music gig, and I really wasn't interested. The prospect
of singing Top 40 dance music left me cold, but Paul, being the
pragmatic one, kept insisting that some work was better than no

work. However, after that horrendous experience with the drunken girl singer and the biker gang, I stuck to my guns, and Paul dug deep and found me some work.

Discos were coming on the scene, and the live music landscape was changing very fast. Even though I was only around twenty-one years old, I had been working hard and had been building a rather nice reputation as a quality jazz singer, especially with the finer musicians in Los Angeles. I was proud of the fact that I was working with highly regarded players, and that between my hard work, and Paul's effective promotion of me, my reputation was growing. If it meant working less to sing the music I loved, I was willing to sacrifice quantity for quality. At that time, the great band leader Gerald Wilson had a call-in radio talk show on L.A.'s jazz station, 103.1. He always had wonderful guests on his show, and one day, he had on one of my favorite singers, Johnny Hartman. Johnny Hartman was a singer I listened to a lot in those days. I loved his phrasing, the slow, rolling way he'd move into his next note or word or phrase. Harmonically, he was more adventurous than Sinatra or Tony Bennett or many of the other singers I studied and admired, and I remember looking forward all that morning to Gerald Wilson's noontime show with Mr. Hartman.

When the show came on, I listened excitedly as they shared stories of their experiences in show business, and when Mr. Wilson invited listeners to call in with questions and comments for Mr. Hartman, on a lark, I called in and was surprised when the show's producer asked me, "Are you Pete Marino, the singer here in town?" I couldn't believe that he'd even heard of me! The producer of The Gerald Wilson Radio Show! He asked me to hold for a minute and said he'd put me on the air. Man, was I ever excited! I kept my radio on in the kitchen, but I had to talk on my bedroom phone in order to avoid feedback, so I could barely hear, but unbelievably, there was Gerald Wilson, on 103.1, the greatest jazz station ever, saying that he had a wonderful local jazz singer on the line, Pete Marino, calling in to talk to him and Johnny Hartman! You could have knocked me over with a feather! And the funny part is, I had no idea what I was going to say! I do remember telling them both how much I respected and enjoyed their work, and, was so honored that they took my call. Now the real icing on the cake was, Johnny Hartman was performing that night at the Parisian Room in Los Angeles, and he invited me to be his guest at the show!

What a night! I had never been to the Parisian Room. It was in a predominantly black neighborhood and my date and I were, as far as I recall, the only white people there. We arrived early; I wanted to meet Mr. Hartman before he began his show. The man at the door turned out to be very nice but looked at us quizzicality as we approached. It wasn't a big stretch to think that maybe we were lost, but upon giving him my name, he immediately said that Mr. Hartman had left instructions. We were led to a front-row table, off to the side, and we were immediately the center of attention. I must say that having been raised in San Pedro, I was brought up with people from all races, religions, both rich and poor. I've never been one to judge by skin color or things like that, but being, I think, the only two white people in this very crowded club that night seemed, at first, oddly intimidating. Perhaps I was feeding of my companion's insecurities and my excitement of meeting and hearing Johnny Hartman, but when we first got in the club, it was intense, oddly so, because I'd never felt this before.

That feeling changed abruptly when Mr. Hartman himself came strolling over to the table and extended his hand to me with a warm greeting. I stood, and we exchanged hellos, introduced him to my date, and he sat with us for a couple of minutes. Oh, yeah, we were certainly the center of attention now, but now, everything was cool, but you could tell that everyone in the room was wondering who the hell we were. Johnny Hartman was a gentleman. He asked if I would like to sing a song, and of course I jumped at the chance. You guessed it, "Summertime!" Just called the key to the band, counted out the rhythm, and pow! From a chance phone call to talking with the great Gerald Wilson and Johnny Hartman to singing at his show... And really learning that music and life IS and SHOULD be colorblind...Yeah, WHAT A NIGHT!

Here I was, a young man, enjoying the crazy and hypnotic scene that was the music business in Hollywood, and I was a part of it! When I wasn't singing, I was out watching other singers or musicians I admired, and I was getting to know who was, who. I was rubbing elbows with record producers, actors, movie stars—celebrities of all kinds. It seemed everywhere I went there was some kind of star or another; it's just the way it was. It might sound strange, but at the time, it was a common occurrence to hang out with a household name or a big producer at a club or a party. That was the magic of Hollywood and show business.

I was also learning that knowing the right people was valuable. Relationships were currency, and due to my experiences through the golf tour and music, I found myself with a wide range of friends and acquaintances. I wasn't so much aware of this as was my manager, Paul. With the onslaught of discos, my bookings were dwindling. Paul was hounding me to do a Top 40 dance show, and I'd rather have driven a truck! We were constantly at odds over it. I was after him to get me jazz gigs, which were few and far between, and he wanted me to go for the low-hanging fruit; dance gigs! It was a tough time for me. It truly seemed as if I was close to making a breakthrough. I was making a nice, albeit local, name for myself. I was respected by L.A.'s top musicians as a singer. I was on a first-name basis with many record producers and sound engineers, TV and movie stars... it just seemed like I was climbing the ladder, and then POW! Nightclubs and piano bars were being remodeled overnight into discos, shrinking my market considerably. Fortunately, the relationships that I had built brought with them opportunities to make a buck or two, and I was able to supplement my flagging performance income.

Chapter 3

STREET HUSTLE

Chance, fate, luck, call it what you will. It's funny how there's a string that somehow ties people and events together, making sense of situations that at the time seem to have no relationship to one another. Looking back, that's how it all seems. As my bookings, and therefore my income lessened, I found myself almost naturally connecting people I knew together. For instance, a band I knew I got booked at a club, and then I introduced them to a record producer who got them signed to a record label, and I was paid a finder's fee. I really didn't know what I was doing, but I just kept my ears open and kept putting people and situations together. I was constantly busy—don't ask me how. One opportunity presented itself after another. Not

32

all, mind you, worked out! But I was so busy, I wasn't bothering Pau about my sporadic singing gigs. I was having fun!

One project that stood out was a jazz cello player I was trying to get a record deal for. He was a wonderful talent named Mike Jacobsen. We called him Jake. Jake played cello and sax as a sideman at the time for Smokey Robinson. Smokey had only the best, so you know Jake was top caliber.

I was producing Jake with a great engineer and producer named Sy Mitchell. I had been showcasing Jake around town, finally doing a show at Howard Rumsey's "Concerts by the Sea." Howard Rumsey was another great jazz talent who was also a fine gentleman that was so kind to me as a young man; he allowed me to use his beautiful club on the Redondo Beach Pier to showcase Jake to some record company executives. Sy Mitchell and I, thanks largely to Howard Rumsey, got some interest that night and went on to record Jake. Sy and I booked time at Warner Brothers Studios, and on the afternoon of my twenty-first birthday, I, along with my close pal Rocco Presutti, pulled into the studio parking lot and parked beside four Rolls-Royce sedans, all lined up in different colors. These belonged to the Jacksons, who were also in the studio that night. Joan Baez was in studio A, and Bill Withers was in a mixing session. Exciting way to spend my twenty-first birthday! We spent the entire evening recording Mike Jacobson's jazz cello trio playing Jake's original music. After the session, Rocco and I went in search of my first LEGAL drink, and Sy took off with the tapes. He had another studio where, over the next few days, he mixed the tapes. Sy had been wanting to record me, so during this time, he had me bring a trio into this studio and we laid down three songs. A few weeks later we met with Al Levin at Blue Note Records, who had shown interest in the Mike Jacobson project.

As we sat in the meeting at Blue Note playing Jake's tape for Mr. Levin, it became clear very quickly that Mr. Levin was losing interest. Sensing this, Sy got up and told him to stop the tape. When the music stopped, Sy asked what was wrong. Mr. Levin said that he's had second thoughts about signing a jazz cello player, because there was already a jazz violinist out there doing quite well, and he thought that that was enough. He was referring to Stephane Grappelli. Without skipping a beat, Sy pulled another tape out of his briefcase and said, "Well then, so as not to waste our time, put this on. This'll get ya!" As Mr. Levin is loading the tape up, Sy gave me a wink. I had no idea what was going on, and all of a sudden, over the speakers in this big mucky-muck's office I hear myself singing "When Sunny Gets Blue"! Mr. Levin sat back in his chair, lit a big, stinky cigar, and listened. I'll be damned! He liked it! Sy snuck this in on both of us. Now, I'm trying to be cool, because at this point, he doesn't know it's me singing. He listens a bit more, then fast-forwards and spot-checks the next two songs, turned off the tape and asked, "Who's that singer?" Sy just smiled and pointed to me. Mr. Levin, who was a large, grumpy and somewhat imposing fellow, for the first time since we'd started our meeting, managed a smile. Here I was, with a first-rate producer in the office of a big-time record company executive, and we're starting to talk about a record deal for me! I had walked in forty-five minutes before to pitch another artist, had no inkling that Sy even had my tapes, and here I was, listening to Sy Mitchell pitch me to Blue Note! Unbelievable! Only in Hollywood! Mr. Levin wanted to take some time to consider things, so Sy made a follow-up appointment with him and we left.

I was on cloud nine! I asked Sy what possessed him to try that. He said that he learned a long time ago to have a backup plan, and in this case, I was it! But he didn't think he'd need it, because he really thought that he was going to buy Jake's project, but he brought my tape along, just in case. Blue Note took a pass on my project, too—but it sure was exciting and encouraging to be considered by such a stellar producer and wonderful record label. I was honored and disappointed, too.

Chapter 4

NO VISIBLE MEANS OF SUPPORT

About this time, the financial industry created a business around a tax loophole which utilized master recordings (albums) as an investment. My manager Paul's background in the New York Stock Exchange led to him being contacted by a Wall Street entrepreneur named Herman Finesod. Herman partnered with Paul in this "tax shelter" business, and together they formed Jackie Resources, Inc., an investment company. Paul ran the West Coast operation. And although he certainly had established contacts throughout the music industry, Paul thought that I would be an asset in that regard. He felt that I could use my contacts, and his, to license the master recordings needed as the investment product, leaving him free to run the business and seek high-dollar investors. This opportunity fit right in with the direction things were going for me. I was eager to learn the "business" side of show business, and the prospect of licensing music was exciting. I started right away, for $200 per week plus some expenses, plus an override on the business I brought in, both the music I licensed and any clients I brought in. The offices were right on Sunset Boulevard—6464 Sunset Blvd., The Stanley Folb Building. It was top drawer all the way.

Paul was evidently in his element. He was constantly on the phone promoting this wonderful tax-saving opportunity to anyone and everyone who would listen. What a salesman he was! It is no wonder that he retired from Wall Street at such a young age; with his energy and his rap, he could sell almost anyone anything. He was non-stop, call after call, meeting after meeting. I'd never seen anything like it! While Paul was developing a sales force and clientele, I was looking for master recordings (albums) that we could purchase the rights to. I was contacting artists and artist managers; recording engineers and record producers who I had met along the way. I'd take them to lunch or dinner on my expense account, which made me look and feel like a real big shot. My ability to wine and dine my product sources was by design, and this little investment really paid off. Word spread like wildfire throughout the record-producing community that I, as a buyer for Jackie Resources, Inc., was a stand-up guy who was willing and able to pay good money for a wide variety of recorded music.

This new tax shelter business created a need for recorded music that until now hadn't existed, and there was a loud buzz throughout Hollywood. People in all corners of the industry were talking, and, even though I was brought into it mostly because my manager couldn't get me singing work, I found myself becoming an important player. My phone was ringing like crazy from people who'd heard of me from so and so, and, within a couple of months of being open for business, I found myself working twelve-hour days or more! I was meeting artists and producers and listening to music nonstop, it seemed, and negotiating to buy this music on behalf of the company. Paul, too, had his sources for music product, which he would turn over to me to handle the initial phases of qualifying and evaluation.

One day, after returning from lunch, I was standing at the reception desk reading phone messages when a man emerged from Paul's office, which was at the end of a long hallway. He came at me at nearly a full run, with an armful of 16ips tape boxes. He literally slammed them into my chest, proclaiming in a loud, obnoxious voice, "You, put these on, right now! Paul wants to hear them— now!" As the phone messages scattered to the floor, the normally mild-mannered me responded in kind to this belligerent stranger who had just bruised my chest with these boxes of tapes.

"Fuck You! Who do you think you are, telling me what to do!" And I shoved the tapes back in his arms and marched into Paul's office. I was pissed! Everyone in the office was startled by my reaction, because they had never seen me be anything but cordial. But this guy had just really pushed my buttons and had reminded me that in spite of the expense account and the fancy friends and clients I was wining and dining, in the offices of Jackie Resources, Inc., I was only a glorified office boy.

It was also the very unlikely beginning of a lifelong friendship.

This man, Jack Millman, had been waiting with Paul for some time for me to return from lunch so I could cue up the tapes that Jack had for sale. I was the only one who knew how to operate the equipment, so that was the reason for his impatient approach. Jack had a company named Music Industries, which supplied the film business with background music, and he had a huge library of recorded music. At this point, all I knew of him was that he was a big-mouthed, rude

S.O.B. and I wanted nothing to do with him. But to Paul, he was an extremely important source of inventory, the biggest single source and here I was, telling this V.I.P. to go screw himself...completely out of character. As I stormed into his office, Paul first looked at me in shock, and then after a stunned moment, he burst out in laughter Through his laughter, he tried to tell Jack (who had followed me into his office), to apologize to me but he couldn't control his laughter. This finally got Jack to laughing, which only pissed me off more! I stomped down the hall to my office, soon to be followed by Paul and Jack. After the requisite apologies, I allowed my bruised ego to heal and we got on with business.

Jack Millman was a major supplier of master recordings to Jackie Resources, Inc., and during the next year, we became good friends, a friendship that has lasted over forty years.

JACK MILLMAN

By then I had been with Jackie Resources, Inc., just over a year. During that time, I made a lot of connections in the music business and related fields. One weekend, I had the opportunity to go to Palm Springs. I was visiting a man I had recently met who was a retired record distributor named Lenny Garmisa. I was hoping to develop new sources of master recordings. Lenny was originally from Chicago and had been one of the largest "rack-jobbers" (record distributors) in the music business. His Palm Springs home was filled with pictures of himself with famous singers and stars whose records he had distributed, but the most proudly placed were those of himself with Frank Sinatra.

He told me of his long friendship with Mr. S., even saying that their friendship was a big factor in his decisions to retire in Palm Springs. After hearing this, I shared my Sinatra stories, which he found pretty charming. We had finished our meeting and I was preparing to leave when Lenny asked if I could stay a few minutes more—someone was stopping by in a few minutes that he'd like me to say hello to.

Not long after the doorbell rang, Lenny opened the door and the guest says, "Hello, Shirts!" You see, Lenny's last name, Garmisa, in Italian, loosely means, "shirts." That was the nickname given him by Frank Sinatra! Lenny was standing in the entryway with Frank Sinatra! He said his hellos and told Mr. S. to come in and say hello to a mutual pal. I was pretty sure Lenny was testing me to see if I knew Sinatra at all, or if I was just another B.S. artist from Hollywood. As Sinatra came in the room, he smiled and came to me with his hand out to shake and said, "Hello, Petey!" I was pretty sure he'd recognize me, because he had a couple of times before, but he remembered my name—again! That always blew my mind! It's not like we really knew each other or that our run-ins were so impressive (except to me), but he always immediately recognized me and called me by name and always followed with "How's your father?" Then he said something like, "Man, you sure do get around! How do you guys know each other?" I told him that I was asking Lenny for sources of recordings that I could buy or license.

During my earlier meeting with Lenny, he was interested but noncommittal, and I was to schedule a follow-up meeting. But seeing as I passed the "Sinatra" test, he now spoke in favor of it and me and said he would help me. Mr. Sinatra offered to arrange a meeting with me and Ernie Freeman of Motown Records. He felt that Ernie would be a good person for me to know. That meeting with Ernie Freeman took place about a week later. I met him for lunch at the Jolly Roger on Sunset. Motown's offices were three blocks from ours, and the Jolly Roger was halfway between for both of us. Mr. S. was right, as Ernie was a great guy to know. Through him, I was put in touch with many opportunities. Thank you, Lenny, for keeping me around that day to say hello to Mr. S., to Mr. S. for the call and referral to Ernie Freeman, and to Ernie, for so many introductions and kindnesses.

One introduction was to another close friend of Frank Sinatra's, the great pianist and Sinatra' rehearsal pianist and singer, Frankie Randall. Frankie was a friendly and fun guy. He also knew everyone in show business, and everyone loved Frankie! He put me in touch with many people and opportunities, from Steve Allen to Jack Jones. We played a lot of golf and had a lot of fun and enjoyed a friendship until his death in 2014.

Getting back to when I was coming up in Hollywood... I was a young guy with a few bucks in a fast town, not always a good combination. A salesman for Jackie Resources, Inc., Marty Allred and I started running together. I never met anyone like Marty. He looked like a combination of Fred Astaire and David Niven; long and lanky with movements that glided, like Astaire, and facial features similar to David Niven's. The effect was that strangers immediately felt comfortable with him and somehow trusted him as if they'd known him all their lives. Funny, always up, always the life of the party, dressed to the nines, slick, smooth as silk, so much fun to be with—and the biggest con man I've ever met! But you'd forgive him all of it, he was that likable (and a cokehead to boot!).

Marty had just quit being a rather successful musician. He was an incredible drummer, and had worked for Glen Campbell and Roger Miller, to name only a couple. He was a great musician, but he wanted more, and being a drummer had its ceiling. Sales was his calling, as he certainly had the gift of gab, and grift! As I said, hanging with Marty was more fun than I'd ever had. He was one of those people who "never met a stranger"; everywhere we went seemed to be a party or led to one. The only problem was, I was always picking up the tab! I was young and naïve and having such a good time I really didn't care. He introduced me to cocaine, and all of its highs and lows, and for a while, I jumped right in.

We hit all the hot spots in Hollywood and Beverly Hills, hung out with stars and partied like there was no tomorrow. But tomorrow came, and I didn't care. Like I said, I was having too much fun! Marty and I had many adventures on and off over a five-year period. I hate to admit it, but I was in awe of Marty. Maybe twenty-five years my senior, he was tall and well dressed. He always seemed in control of himself and every situation. He knew all the "right" people and we went to all the hip places. Marty was as cool as anyone I'd ever known. I was honored to be his wingman. We did crazy stuff. He was selling for Jackie Resources and I was doing the licensing for the company as well as hustling my side deals (as Marty did also), but neither of us was punching a clock. We'd often get together around 3:00 pm at the Jolly Roger bar and have a drink or two while we'd plan the evening of dinner and drinks. However, this rarely included dinner because on the way to dinner we'd usually stop and buy some coke, and away we'd go, bar to club to bar to party until 1:00 or 2:00 am. You'd think that we were out chasing girls, and yes, that sometimes would happen. Our real purpose was to mingle: to meet people, reconnect with people. Find out who's doing what, where, and to whom. Connecting people to each other was really the thing. Marty didn't just work the room, he worked the town. He was nonstop, and people were attracted to him like moths to flame. It was exciting. Crazy, and I was learning a lot, including all the wrong things. Good thing I've always been such a coward. I didn't have the nerve or the imagination to twist details up or even outright lie. But I have to admit that many times I stood by and watched as Marty worked a "prospect," knowing the whole time that whatever Marty was selling wasn't worth the breath it took to tell the story. Yet I stood by in amazement. He was like one of those characters in that great Paul Newman and Robert Redford movie The Sting. I met lots of characters through Marty, and had laughs like I can't describe, but he was trouble. One day we were going into Musso and Frank's for a late lunch and we ran into Nelson Riddle, who, in my opinion, then and now, was one of the world's greatest arrangers. The arrangements that he wrote for Sinatra were my favorites. I had such great respect for him, and here I was, being introduced to him by Marty. Marty knew him from recording session work and asked him to join us, which, I'm happy to say, he did. I was very familiar with Nelson Riddle's work. I was surprised at how humble, embarrassed really, he became when I complimented him on his work. Once he recognized that I was truly knowledgeable about his work, and that I knew Mr. Sinatra and the work they had done together, he relaxed a bit. What an honor. So, because of Marty, I had lunch with Nelson Riddle. I never saw him again, but, wow!

On the other hand, one night we ended up at the house of Billie Campbell, Glen's former wife. Marty knew her from the days he worked for Glen. That night, she was having a cocktail party.

The next afternoon, Marty and I drove back to Billie Campbell's house. As we pulled up, I asked what we're doing there, and he told me he was picking up a potted plant from her front porch that she left out for him, and that he needed my help putting it in his trunk. I went along with it, only to find out months later that he saw it as we had left the party the night before and wanted it, so he went back and STOLE IT! I was pissed! I couldn't imagine Marty just helping himself to Billie's property! And so nonchalantly! Now I had a different view of Marty. But to give you an idea...one day it's Nelson Riddle, and the next it's, grand larceny! More Marty to come.

I mentioned earlier that I went to work at Jackie Resources, Inc., for $200 a week plus a percentage of what master recordings or investment clients I brought in, and that I was young and naïve. I never got that in writing. I trusted Paul. He was my manager and had always protected me. I never even thought to have a contract, and if it weren't for Herman Finesod, I never would have needed one.

The end of the year came—a very successful one, I might add—and there was no percentage for me...a percentage that would have been worth about $60,000! Paul could only fight so hard without damaging his position; I understood. Herman wasn't going to honor a verbal agreement. Paul gave me a nice "bonus," hoping to appease me, but I quit. I don't like being screwed. I realized that I had set myself up for it, by not having a written agreement, but I had no respect for Herman. Cheating me out of what was no kind of money to him, just because he could. I couldn't leave fast enough. I had a few bucks, because I had been working my side deals, but now I had no idea of what to do. I remember feeling like I'd lost my best friend when I said goodbye to Paul. I drove home feeling very dejected

The last year or so had brought some big and exciting changes to my life, changes that I never anticipated but had come to enjoy. I never thought I'd be on the business side of show business, yet here I was, and loving it. Sure, I missed singing and performing, but the music licensing business was interesting, and the contacts were incredible,

44

and the deal-making and general hustle was both exciting and lucrative. I was feeling like I was going to lose it all by being so far away. I wasn't home ten minutes before the phone rang.

It was Jack Millman.

I was living in a beautiful two-bedroom apartment that was high on a hilltop in San Pedro. It had a clear view east to downtown Los Angeles and south overlooking L.A. Harbor. I shared it with my dear friend and great musician Rocco Presutti. About a year prior to this, Rocco had stopped by and asked if he could stay the weekend; he was having some domestic difficulties. That weekend and those difficulties stretched out and he'd been at my apartment ever since! We joke about that to this day! Anyway, my office and all of my business was in Hollywood and the surrounding areas. As I made the fifty-minute drive from the Jackie Resources, Inc., offices to my home in San Pedro that afternoon, I remember thinking how isolated I was going to be living so far from the action. Besides the fact that it was my hometown, one of the main reasons I liked living there was that I could get away from everything.

But being away all the time was a different story. I was trying to figure a way to get an office. I remember this clearly. I was concerned that I could lose ground quickly if I wasn't visibly "on the scene." I was not happy with what had happened with Paul and Herman, and I was worried about my future. I had been making more money on the side than I did from my salary, which was why the year-end percentage participation was so important. Remember, I was only drawing $200 per week, plus approved expenses. Now that I no longer had the use of an office in town, and all that goes with it, plus with the loss of the "percentage," I had to come up with something quick. Sure, I remember that ride home, which is why I remember that I wasn't home ten minutes when Jack Millman called.

Jack was all amped up! He was so happy and excited that I had quit Jackie Resources! Here I was, Mr. Melancholy, and he's going on about how great this is! It turns out that he had this grand idea for us to team up, combine resources, and start our own music licensing company. With his music library and clients, and my sources for new music product and our combined experience, the idea had merit. I spent the next six months or so operating out of the Jolly Roger on Sunset during the day, and Martoni's Restaurant late afternoon and evenings. These were my offices. Not ideal, but not unheard of in my "no visible means of support" existence. Mind you, there was nothing illegal going on, except drug use, perhaps. (I don't mean to sound cavalier about the drugs here, but at the time, in Hollywood, coke was everywhere. I just introduced people and situations that resulted in my being paid. I ran things rather informally, that's all.)

The hours, as you might guess, were anything but fixed; lots of meetings coincided with meals and or cocktails. I'd learned from one of the best, Mr. Marty Allred, how to use social settings for meetings as well as places to create new clients. Lots of early starts, and lots of late nights. Not a good schedule without an office, especially when you live nearly an hour's drive away. Even though I was in my mid-twenties, it was wearing on me even with the occasional illegal lift, and as much as I loved that great place in San Pedro, it was time to look for a place in town.

During this time, Jack and I pursued the idea of joining forces. We did deals together, but I didn't want to partner up with anybody. I was busy working on all types of projects with all kinds of people, even singing now and then, and the variety was intoxicating to me. The long drive, however, was a problem. One day, Jack called and said he had the answer to all my problems; all I had to do was take care of some flowers. It turned out that his former wife had moved to Venezuela for two years, leaving Jack in charge of watering her prize roses and orchids, as well as maintaining the house for her. The house was a small two-bedroom, two- bath, Spanish-style bungalow in the old Hollywood flats, right in the heart of town. I wasn't sure I'd heard him right, so I asked Jack to repeat the terms of the house rental again. He told me, "Just make sure you don't kill those fucking flowers. She's crazy and she loves those fucking flowers!"

"But how much money per month" I asked.

"No money! Just don't let those flowers die!"

How 'bout that?! As soon as I could, I left San Pedro and took Jack up on that deal, which sounded so good. You know the kind, the one that may be too good to be true?

The prize roses didn't give me too much trouble. There were four or five different, beautiful types of rose bushes lining the walkways, and even more on each side of the stoop. The orchids, on the other hand, seemed to die when I simply walked by them. In the rear of the house, off of the kitchen was a sunroom. This room had a small table and two chairs that were positioned to best take in the view of the many orchids that lined the perimeter of the room. There must have been twenty different plants growing. The air was heavy with their scent. I wasn't a big fan of the smell, but they were pretty. And remember, Jack had stressed how important the roses and the orchids were to his former wife. Because of this, I knew those flowers were ill-fated. I had been living there about a month or so when I called Jack to tell him that I was killing the orchids. I had been following the instructions to the letter; the roses were doing fine, but the orchids were hopeless!

47

Later that day, he stopped by and showed me where the names of the types of orchids were written in a journal and said that we would buy new plants before his ex-wife returned.

Okay, I was happy to replace them, glad to know what they were so that I could replace them. And so, I relaxed. Heck, I had nearly two years before she was coming back; two years before I had to move, and before I had to meet her. Jack had told me many stories about his crazy former wife. Her name was Ludmila, a beautiful and fiery Russian immigrant who had burned down their house one day following an argument. And that was only one of many stories Jack reveled in telling. Let's say she was a bit caustic. From everything Jack had told me about Ludmila, she sounded pretty scary. Trust me, I was in no hurry to meet her. The next five months or so were great. I had gotten used to living alone and to living in Hollywood. Being right in town certainly had its perks: no more long drives to and from home and to and from meetings, plus, my house doubled as my office. Everything was clicking along.

One night, around 11:00 pm, I was awakened by a woman and a young man coming into the house. They had let themselves in through the front door with a key, and as I entered the living room, the woman dropped her luggage and quickly backpedaled in surprise as she exclaims "Who da fuck are you!" in a frightened and heavily accented voice. "What are you doing in my house?" As she's yelling at me, the young man with her, who looked like he was from Latin America, started to position himself between us—threateningly!

"I'm Peter, Jack's friend! He asked me to watch the house while you were in South America! Didn't he tell you?" She reached over and put a hand on the young man's shoulder, stopping him, and said no, Jack had never mentioned anything about anyone staying at her house.

I was able to get her to let me call Jack, and after much yelling and screaming, she handed me the phone. Jack! I can't believe he never told her! Here I am at 11:30 at night, dressed only in my boxers, standing in the house of a lady who has no idea who I am, and I thought I had a place to live for another year and a half.

And then it hit me—the orchids were all dead! I didn't get a chance to replace them. I had just heard how crazy she could be when she was yelling at Jack on the phone. I knew I was in trouble! And the way she was controlling this young man like he was a well-trained servant. I was just waiting for her to sic him on me—and he was waiting for the command. This lady was scary. All I wanted was OUT, but since I was standing there in just my underwear, there really wasn't anywhere to go.

The next few months were crazy. I went from living peacefully in this cool little house, enjoying the newness and quiet of living alone to having to share the place with this raving lunatic and her endless stream of friends and lovers partying nonstop. Ludmila was maybe in her late thirties, stone cold crazy, but she was also a stunning woman. The original party girl, she could be charming and coy, or cold and ruthless. She, at her very core, wanted to love everything and everyone, and really was well intentioned.

The fact that she had uncontrollable anger issues that could turn extremely violent, to me, outweighed her alluring looks and otherwise charming ways. One of the reasons Jack divorced her was that she burned down their house to settle an argument! Like I said, she was nuts! But that was also part of her charm. When I said earlier that she wanted to love everybody, well, she tried! She had so many lovers, more lovers than anyone I'd ever known, and a few famous ones. Peter Graves would drop in now and then, and David Carradine was a frequent visitor. The first time I met David I was awakened by loud knocking late one night. I pulled on some pants and went down the hall, turned on the porch light, and opened the door only to see the profile of some guy pissing off the porch—right onto Ludmila's prize rose bushes! I yelled something at him to make him stop, and he drunkenly stumbled and turned, still peeing, IN MY DIRECTION! I jump out of the way, wide awake now, realizing who it was just as he stopped his stream and zipped up and asked for Ludmila. At this point, Ludmila, who had heard the commotion, showed up, found the scene very amusing, and half carried David back to her room. There was always something going on. If Ludmila was in town, there was always something going on, and her action was starting to mix in with my friends and business. Before long, my old pal Marty even found his way into Ludmila's lair. The whole time she's partying with these guys, her houseman, Fernando, was waiting on everybody hand and foot, but I could see his resentment building. He rarely spoke, and when he did, it was always in Spanish and in very hushed tones. This guy was wired. It was obvious that he was in love with Ludmila. She introduced him as her houseboy but treated him as her slave. They had a strange relationship. I suspected she gave him some sort of satisfaction, but only suspected. Anyway, Fernando did not like me at all. From that first night, he would lurk about and seem to spy on me—it was really creepy. Even though I wasn't playing house with Ludmila, he behaved toward me as if he was jealous. Maybe because I had a room, and she made him sleep in the garage!

Man, that was one wild scene, way too wild for me. After a few months, I had to get out. All the people coming and going all hours of the day and night, plus this zombie Fernando hanging around and now Ludmila was making it a game to get me in bed, and although she was certainly attractive, I knew it would be trouble. Yes, even at that young age, I had some brains! One day, out of the blue, she started acting and talking like we were lovers—real coquettish, playful. She said she made dinner reservations for us the next night, which happened to be Valentine's Day. I told her that I had plans, and just kind of jokingly brushed it off. The next afternoon, I was at the house of movie producer Marty Hornstein. We spent the day just hanging out and I completely forgot the conversation with Ludmila from the day before. I drove up to the house about 8:30 that evening and went inside to find Ludmila simmering in a chair next to a raging fire in the fireplace. Behind her, standing menacingly with his arms folded across his chest, was a stern and angry Fernando. I was greeted with her heavily accented voice hissing at me hatefully, "Where have you been? How dare you," as her voice rose, "forget me! Stand ME UP! ON VALENTINE'S DAY!"

Well, then I remembered. This lady was nuts! She really meant it. Then she went on to tell and show me what was in the fire: all my music charts, my musical arrangements, and some of my clothes! As I reacted, she ordered Fernando to ATTACK! Finally, he got his chance to get at me, and he wasn't wasting a moment! I managed to fend him off enough to get to my car, get in, close the door, start it and put it in gear, and take off down the street. My car had running boards, and the driver's window was down. Fernando stood on the running board as I drove away and reached in and punched me repeatedly through the open window causing me to crash into a light pole, hitting my head on the steering wheel and getting knocked out. I came to on the sidewalk flat on my back with Ludmila on top of me, punching me in the face!

Just then, my dear friend Douglas Foxworthy rushed in and broke up this bizarre ordeal. This was sheer luck. Douglas was a multi-talented songwriter and playwright, as well as a record producer, who lived in San Diego, not Hollywood. I had no idea that he was in town, let alone planning to drop by; that's why I say it was sheer luck! He pulled her off of me and calmed her down. They had come to like each other. Douglas frequently visited me to discuss business, and he and Ludmila got along well. He was another guy that resisted her siren calls, which made her all the more friendly to him. He was happily married, and, I think, didn't need the complications although I do think he enjoyed the interplay. Anyway, I was dazed, so he took me and a few of my possessions to Marty's house until I could find a place to live. To this day, I credit Douglas with saving my life.

A few days later I collected my bruised car and the rest of my things from that lunatic's house. In hindsight, staying at Marty's wasn't a great idea either, but at the time, it seemed as normal an existence as any. I was completely welcome there and we immediately settled on a routine. Mornings began around 7:00. I'd leave the guest room to shower and dress while Marty made coffee and often breakfast. We'd eat and plan our days which, as had been the case in the Jackie Resources days, now included meeting later in the afternoon to have a drink and warm up for the evening. And, just like in the Jackie Resources days, we'd pick up a gram or two of coke. After coffee and breakfast, we'd go our separate ways. We were both doing basically the same thing: he was selling tax shelters and any other investment-related product he could, and I was licensing music and music-related films and putting people and opportunities together. In other words, we were out hustling every day. Different products, same M.O. No guarantee. No nothing. Ingenuity, creativity, and hard work. No safety nets at all, until I went to work for Jack Millman and actually got a paycheck!

We were both pretty good at what we did. Anyway, we'd meet after a hard day and call Ed. Ed was Marty's primary coke dealer. Ed was a short, average-built man of Armenian descent who was usually in a foul mood and smelled of too much Aramis cologne. Marty had many names for Ed: Fast Eddie, Biscuits (because his coke was so heavily cut it sometimes looked like flour), or my favorite, The Marquis de Toot! Marty's war cry would be "Call Ed!" And off we'd go to Eddie's house to score our magic powder. Ed's was always an interesting place. His clientele consisted of a few of Hollywood's up-and-comers, from gold-digging starlet types right up to the A-list stars and businessmen the starlets were hoping to know. It was always an adventure going to Ed's, who lived across town in the Silverlake district. I admit, I liked the high, but the whole scene around scoring, making the call, arguing with Ed about what time to come by his house, hustling to the bank to get cash before it closed (there were no ATMs in those days), fighting the cross-town traffic while full of anticipation of that first, fat line, getting to Ed's and mixing in with the others in the "inner circle" of uptown derelicts as I waited to get the goods. The real romance was in the chase of the score, not so much in the high, but the combination was a bitch—and I was becoming as addicted as Marty.

I'd planned to stay at Marty's only for a few days, but he liked the company and I had nowhere really to go, so a few days quickly turned into a few months. He had many acquaintances, and as I mentioned before, Marty was great fun to be around. But due to his being truly without conscience, he had few friends. Seems that sooner or later he's gonna take you down if you hang around long enough. But one friend he had, and that man is still my friend today: Rick Marcelli. Rick had met Marty when they both worked for Roger Miller, and, like me, Rick was charmed by Marty, knew what he was, but liked him anyway. To this day, Rick and I still marvel over Marty stories that we share, knowing full well that no one would understand without knowing him. Marty was one of a kind. Anyway, the three of us would hit the town on occasion. As it turned out, the best thing about knowing Marty was meeting Rick. What a bright guy. Remember the soda cups that 7-Elevens had with the pictures of athletes on them? That was Rick's idea. Also, as their personal manager, he had been responsible for the careers of such greats as Jenny Jones, Shields and Yarnell, and arguably the world's best illusionist, David Copperfield, to name a few.

One night, the three of us went to Don Randi's Baked Potato. Thumbs Carlisle was playing and had invited Marty to sit in, so off we went. Thumbs had worked with Roger Miller, so it was old home week for them, but it was the first time I'd met him. I hung out with everyone on the first break, but felt like a third wheel, so when the second break came, I wandered off and sat at the bar. On one side was an actor I'd met before, Michael Parks, who had a show on TV I liked called Then Came Bronson. Not long after we had started talking, a young woman sat in the empty seat next to me. Michael, immediately put the moves on her, but she wasn't buying. So, without skipping a beat, he turned his attention elsewhere and she and I started a conversation that lasted about a year. Her name was Claudia Previn. Yes, the daughter of Andre, stepdaughter of Mia Farrow, daughter of former band singer Betty Bennett and stepdaughter of jazz guitar virtuoso Mundell Llowe. Heady lineage. Nice girl and she lived a half mile from Ed's! Convenient! Claudia was fun to hang with. She liked jazz, didn't want a husband, liked to hit the town with Marty and me, just kept things loose. She worked at A&M Records and had herself together. Well, after a while, I got an apartment in San Pedro, and was splitting time between Marty's, Claudia's and my new hideaway in San Pedro. I say "hideaway" because that's just what it was. Nobody from town came there...no one was invited or had the phone number...it was my escape. In "Pedro" I had my hometown friends and family. In

Hollywood, I had a different lifestyle, and I liked, for the most part, to keep them separate.

A year or so after Claudia and I started seeing each other, as casual as it was, we found ourselves drifting apart. For me, it seemed that Marty was there to comfort her, but that may have been my imagination. Knowing Marty, I'm pretty sure she got all the comfort she would need. Marty kept trying to downplay it, so I figured it had to be. Truth is, it didn't matter. I really liked Claudia, but I wasn't in love. I hoped they were both having a good time. As for me, I was floundering, doing too much coke, too little singing, making a bunch of money (Jack Millman had made me an "honest man" by hiring me for a huge salary and benefits), but still having too little direction in life...

Then Marty and I came up with a Million Dollar Idea! And Professional Video Services, Inc., was born!

Chapter 5

CENTURY CITY TO SIN CITY

Marty had developed a relationship with a young oil millionaire named Pat Kennedy. Pat was maybe forty years old, a good-looking Irishman who had just made many, many millions in the oil business, and was raring to invest some of that money in anything that looked like fun. Marty wined and dined Pat like there was no tomorrow, as only Marty could. Pretty girls, big stars, fancy parties, you name it, Marty showed Pat the town. When Marty and I came up with the concept for Professional Video Services, Marty knew that Pat Kennedy was the man to go to for the money.

I was licensing music and music-related films, which led us to thinking about medical films as they related to patient education. I did the research and found that medical schools had libraries full of teaching films that could be adapted to our purpose: patient education. We offered videos of various medical procedures to educate patients and rented the video equipment as well as the patient education films to the doctors. We licensed the films from the schools, packaged them and rented them to our end users, the doctors. Once we sold Pat on the idea, we leased a forty-foot motor home, outfitted it to accommodate the video equipment (which, in those days was quite large), and set it up as a viewing room. I would drive the "mobile viewing room" to our appointments and bring the doctor's office manager out to the motor home for the presentation. The concept was an overwhelming success; however, due to the size of the video equipment and the space required to accommodate a patient education viewing room, we went bust within a year. Pat believed so much in this idea that he had leased the motor home, given us office space in his suite of offices on the twentieth floor of the Twin Towers in Century City (complete with membership to the Playboy Club), and hearty salaries on top of that! During that year, fifteen months really if you count the initial startup time we had with salaries before we moved into the offices, Marty and I really busted our tails. We believed in this business. We dialed in every aspect of the business: printing, promo materials, the motorhome, the legal and accounting—everything.

Once we were underway, we had the best editors making our patient videos; we were setting appointments with the top medical, surgical and dental groups; we had the most swanky offices in Century City. We were excited. We all believed that this was such a successful concept and couldn't wait to open the flood gates! The problem was we were way ahead of our time! Due to the expense and the bulkiness of the video equipment, the deal was tough to sell in smaller offices, and lots of doctors had small offices.

At first, everyone we called on received us enthusiastically. As I said, the concept was a huge success. However, with the deal requiring committed office space, most everyone had to consider it carefully. And upon further review... no go. During this time frame, we lived the high life, in more ways than one! Pat, despite the fact that we weren't selling, continued to believe in the project. We would meet to discuss how to improve things often over lunch or dinner at the Playboy Club, which was located at the lobby level of our building. During this time, Pat and Marty went out socially less and less, and although Pat and I didn't go out on the town together, he and I were becoming pals. He lived in Rolling Hills Estates, which sits on a hill above San Pedro. I think this gave us a talking point. He enjoyed Marty's slick, smooth style, but he was more comfortable talking business with me. I liked Pat. He was a regular guy who had hit it big, fast, and hard. He knew he was smart, but he also felt he was a bit lucky. He was a carefree character most of the time, although I saw him put Marty's pants on him a couple of times when Marty was trying to put one past him. Even though he was nice and easygoing, he felt the need to always have his bodyguard present, and I wondered why.

When we finally admitted defeat, Pat took Marty and me to a nice dinner. He wasn't bitter about losing his investment, which was sizable. He felt we gave a great idea all we had, but we were ahead of our time. And we were. Today, you'll find patient education video everywhere, in professional offices and online. We closed up shop and parted friends.

It was during this time that Marty and I met the actor Nick Nolte. One afternoon, Marty issued the daily war cry, "Call Ed!" so after went through all the requisite moves and finally arrived, standing there in Eddie's living room was none other than Nick Nolte, talking to Eddie's niece, Sharon. Sharon had brought Nick by to meet her favorite uncle and to open the door for Nick to join Ed's semi-exclusive insiders club of well-dressed drug-addled derelicts with too much time and money—no secret handshake required. Marty and I had known Sharon for some time. Sharon was a pretty girl, whose most striking feature, along with her very sunny disposition, were her long and shapely legs. In fact, "Legs" became the nickname that later Nolte hung on her. She introduced us to Nick, and we all just hung out for a bit. We all got along great, and after getting what we came for, the four of us hit the town. For the next few months, Nick would meet Marty and me for a meal or a night out on occasion. Sharon and Nick got married, his second marriage, but we weren't invited to the wedding.

I remember one evening I was eating with Nick at the Palm Restaurant and everybody was paying tribute to Nick; he was hot at the time. In the corner was Andy Williams and Pierre Cossette, my old "pals" from my caddying days, and they were getting no attention. Andy kept trying to catch my eye, but I was at just the right angle, so I could get away with ignoring him, when finally, he couldn't stand it any longer. I sensed he had to know what the hell "The Singing Caddy" was doing sitting with Nick "The Heart Throb" Nolte, so finally he walked over and said, "Hi, Pete, how are you?" Well, I'm not proud of it, but he had treated me so poorly... Here I was, with a chance to be mean in return, and I was, telling him, "Hey, Andy, I'm fine, but I'm really busy right now." And I turned to face Nick and resumed my conversation with him as Andy ambled back to his table, shoulders dropped as he shrugged his dismay at Pierre. Andy's ego was bruised; a little by me, but mostly because the civilians in the joint fell over themselves to say hi to Nick or sneak a look at him, and no one was paying him any mind. For my part, I was just dust kicked on his shoes, no big deal really, but I feel bad about that. I've felt bad about that for a long time. Sometimes I can be an ass.

People often ask me what Nick is like. He's just like the guy you see in the movies. Just like that. Is he a good actor? I don't know. Is he a good guy? We had some good times. He always said if I ever needed anything to give him a call, so one day, I did. He had his office on the Paramount lot, and he was HUGE! At the time, it seemed that Nick was the biggest star Hollywood had seen in decades, and he had a lot of power. I was between gigs, so I took him up on his kind offer and I called him for a job. He said he'd get right back to me. I'm still waiting.

After we closed Professional Video Services, Inc., Marty and I went our separate ways. We'd get together on occasion, but for the most part, I needed a break. Running with Marty, even though he was twice my age, was tough! That guy could go eighteen hours a day! Plus, I'd had enough of his game and was tired of footing his bills, so I was back out looking for opportunities. I had been knocking around town for a month or so, with mixed results, as I recall. I was starting to question the choices I'd made and was wishing Nick would call! Here I was, a young man with a considerable amount of experience in things that are either intangible or unmarketable (only in Hollywood), but I somehow carved out a living, not an existence, but usually a damn good living. With the closing of PVS, Inc., and getting the cold shoulder from my "pal" Nick and I'm sure a bunch of other stuff, I was feeling low. As I was reconnecting with people in show business, I was considering getting serious about singing again. I missed the action.

There's a special energy around music and musicians, and actors and television shows and productions and such. And I was missing it. I guess you could say I was feeling lost, disenfranchised. Then one morning the phone rang.

It was Pat Kennedy.

It had been four or five weeks since that goodbye dinner with Marty and Pat, and I was surprised but happy to hear from him. As I mentioned, I really liked Pat. I was surprised by the call because we had concluded our business, and although we were friendly, we really weren't friends. After some catching up, he finally satisfied my curiosity and got down to the reason for his call. It turned out that he had put the money up for a television production that was being shot in Las Vegas, and the producer was avoiding him. Pat told me that he had been trying to get this man on the phone for the last three days, but every time he got stonewalled. He sent someone to Las Vegas to see what was going on and the report was that the "producer" wasn't taking his calls, or doing anything related to the show, because he had been holed up in his hotel room "with a pile of coke and a couple of hookers"!

The show was scheduled to start shooting in ten days. It was a union shoot, and the union contracts were not yet signed. And the artist contracts were not signed. This was a mess, and Pat had a lot of money on the line, and he wanted me to go straighten things out. I told him that I had no television experience, and that I was surprised that he called me. He said he thought I'd be perfect for the job. All he needed was someone who was organized, level-headed, and trustworthy, and he thought that that was me, at least until he talked to Marty. Turns out he called Marty to get my home phone number. When he told Marty the reason for wanting my number, Pat told me that Marty started pitching himself for the gig and completely threw me under the bus! It was at this point, Pat told me, that he stopped thinking that I was right for the gig, and instead KNEW that I was right for it! He wanted me to go to Las Vegas that afternoon. His driver would pick me up and take me to a private jet at Burbank Airport. I'd be met at the airport in Vegas by "MY" limo driver. I would have an exclusive driver, twenty-four hours per day, a suite at the Aladdin Hotel (where the show was shooting), complete food and beverage signing privileges, a more than generous salary and $200 cash per day (Pat jokingly called this my "drug and hooker money," in honor of the man I was sent to fire). In other words, this was a dream deal. It was scheduled to last three weeks, but I was there, working in Vegas for Pat, for nearly a whole year. I did that show, which was the "Penthouse Pet of the Year Awards," and right after that, a show called "The New Faces of Country," and immediately after that, an awards show we'd hoped to do annually in honor of Jimmy Durante called "The Jimmy Awards."

I had been aching for action—and action I got! That year in Las Vegas was a blur of hard work, big fun, high living, and glamorous stars that all seemed to flash by in a minute. I was working with some of the biggest stars in the world: Tony Curtis, Robert Goulet, Liberace, Sammy Davis, Jr., and the list goes on and on...even Professor Irwin Corey! When I wasn't working on a show, I was watching a big Vegas show. Rick Marcelli had his client David Copperfield playing at Caesar's Palace, so we'd meet up, see the show, or a show, or have dinner, and generally hang out. One night we caught George Burns and Peggy Lee, then the next, we were backstage after Ann-Margaret's show. It was like the whole town was open to me. Between the juice that Rick had around town, and that which was generated from my working the shows and knowing other people in town, there wasn't any place I couldn't go—and my money was no good. I was comped all over town! I was never treated so good before or since!

I had a small production office backstage—and I mean small. It must've been ten-by-ten, but it was more like a closet with a desk shoved in it. To make matters worse, it was the center of everything, people coming and going constantly, and usually by the twos and threes! Since the "producer" had been let go, I, by default, was the one left to get things done. With no title or apparent authority, and certainly with no experience, I found myself cleaning up the mess and somehow finding my way. I was getting all the contracts signed, the production details covered, transportation and hotel accommodations and this and that—man, it never stopped! So little had been done that I wasn't even sure what to expect, but I knew to expect some surprises! The first day was fifteen hours of crazy, and the next day was shaping up the same way, and each day after that. Everyone was great at their jobs, from the talent bookers to the crew. They were all top notch. Artie Forrest was directing. He was a real pro. He was, if memory serves, at the time, directing the Academy Awards show. When it came to live television, Artie was top drawer. So, a lot of it was pretty well dialed in, thank God. But I was buried in other stuff, artists contracts and riders, accommodations, union contracts, air and ground transportation, hotel and sponsor agreements... on and on. Pat was calling from L.A. every hour for updates, and everyone on the show was sweating to make things happen according to some kind of schedule.

Everything was behind, of course, including me, when into my tiny office squeezes Jilly Rizzo and Harry Guardino. I knew both of these characters, having met them both before. Harry was a nice guy, always really gracious and cool and was nice to everybody. Jilly, in my humble opinion, was a loudmouth idiot, and he never seemed to care for me. Not that I knew him that well, but every time we bumped into each other, I always felt he treated me like "the help." Anyway, it turned out that Mr. Sinatra was in town and heard that I was involved in this show. He sent his "boys," Jilly and Harry, down to ask me a favor. That favor was to put a singer on the show, a very pretty singer whose name escapes me, but Mr. Sinatra at the time seemed interested in "helping her career." Well, who was I to get in the way of that? So, of course, I agreed to put her on the show. I immediately got with Artie Forrest and the other powers and we reworked the show to accommodate her. I didn't realize it at the time, but Artie was pissed that I did this. About an hour later I got paged to take an urgent call (remember, no cell phones in those days). It was Pat Kennedy. He'd just gotten off of the phone with one of Hollywood's top award-winning television directors, who gave him an earful because a young, wet-behind-the-ears kid just, at the last minute when we are already way behind schedule, restructured the show to accommodate some "girl singer"! I remember Pat asking me, before I could get a word in edgewise, "Why'd you do this, you got a thing for this girl?" I had to let Pat vent for a while. He was having a bad experience with this project, and even though things had been mostly straightened out, he was up against it and had a lot riding on it. Once he simmered down, I was able to explain that I kind of owed Mr. Sinatra a favor or two (he'd introduced me to a Motown Records exec, after all), and I apologized for any inconvenience. He understood. Pat came from the street, I think. At least he always showed that he had street sense, and he did again here. He understood. And he was on his way. He was star struck, and wasn't about to miss this shoot, which had not only lots of stars, but was full of pretty "Penthouse Pets." And Pat was single. Tall, good-looking, rich, and did I mention, single?

This show was a variety show format designed to showcase the Penthouse Pets of the Year in a setting that was homogenized enough to pass as a network television special. To do that, they got a couple of big stars of the day to host and-or perform, mixed in a few jokes and dances and wrapped it all up with sometimes glamorously clad and sometimes barely clad "Pets." We also shot a topless version for foreign distribution and for domestic late-night cable television. Bob Guccione was the publisher of Penthouse magazine. He was also the co-host of the special, sharing those duties with Tony Curtis. Joan Rivers, Robert Goulet, Professor Irwin Corey, a whole bunch of great acts, but all window dressing because in this case, it was about getting the "Pets" on network TV. Because sex sells. Penthouse was expanding into the television and video business, and this was one way that they were doing it.

It really was a pretty good show. I remember a few funny things that happened during this show. We shot this show, "semi-live," meaning that we had a live audience, and we'd do the "take" live, but if it didn't go well, we'd do it again. The pros did their bits like you'd expect, and the Pets did their bits like you'd expect... with a few takes. Also, keep in mind that whenever needed, we were shooting two versions: one with the girls fully clothed and one with them topless.

So, for the aforementioned reason, we were running a couple of hours behind schedule. Robert Goulet arrived on time to do his two numbers. One of the talent coordinators was an old "friend" of his, and to ease the pain of the delay, she took him to the green room. When we called for him, almost two hours later, the two of them showed up so drunk, well, he could barely walk, and she was blushing and giggling like a schoolgirl. Originally the plan was for Mr. Goulet to walk onstage to his musical cue and stand center stage and deliver his two songs, bow, and exit. But with him now barely able to walk, and nobody backstage but me and some stagehands. I had to make a decision. I had the curtain pulled so the audience couldn't see the stage. A stool was placed center stage, and I had Artie adjust the lighting so that a spotlight was on Goulet as he sat on that stool. I then half-carried Goulet out and propped him up on the stool and instructed him to just sit there and do his songs. I'd come back for him when he was done, and the curtain closed. I left the stage... Curtain up, music starts, spotlight hits him, and he sings his ass off! Unbelievable! Beautiful! The audience goes crazy, he smiles that big smile and sits there as the curtain falls, and we run out and catch him as he's slumping, more like melting off the barstool. But he was great!

Later, I was standing in the wings halfheartedly watching a set change when Joan Rivers snuck up behind me and said in my ear in her breathless, excited fashion, "Hey, Pete, what's 10, 9, 8, 7, 6, 5, 4, 3, 2, 1?" "I dunno." She said, "Bo Derek GROWING OLD!" and proceeded to cackle that wonderful cackle of a laugh loudly as she threw her head back in delight. She was thrilled with my reaction to her new joke and was enjoying the moment-and so was I. My very brief time with her was just that, too brief. I could see where she might be a piece of work to deal with in the long run, but we seemed to hit it off and got along really well. What a wonderful woman Joan Rivers was! Funny, clever, always dancing between the lines. I never heard her swear or cuss, innuendo, always, but never crude. She was generous and kind to everyone on the set, never a bad word to or about anyone, except in jest, of course. She was very clever, and as far as I'm concerned, a class act.

Anyway, I was caught up in a whirlwind! This show was crazy. There were a couple of dozen Penthouse Pets running around the casino stirring up all kinds of attention, most of it bad. These were relatively controversial "models," and many of the hotel and casino guests were not impressed by them, specifically their nudity. This was late 1979!

Bob Guccione made sure that he milked everything he could out of the promotional opportunity, so he paraded the women around shamelessly, not just at the Aladdin, but all over town. The prudes were complaining to hotel management, hotel management was trying to appease them because there were a lot of trade-offs for them. The show was bringing the Aladdin a ton of benefits. That same church-going lady from the Midwest who was offended by the behavior of the "Pets" was thrilled to ride the elevator with Tony Curtis, etc., etc. With the TV exposure the show was creating a lot of revenue and promotional streams. So, it had a few rough edges.

It was completely nuts. Just a few days before, I had been lamenting my path. Suddenly, I was in Las Vegas working on a major television special with some of the day's biggest stars, making a bunch of money and literally needing none of it, except to tip, and working fifteen-hour days and enjoying every minute. I had a beautiful one-bedroom suite, a twenty-four hour driver, limo and was surrounded by two dozen exceptionally pretty "Penthouse Pets." Everything would have been perfect if it weren't for those "Penthouse Pets"—well, a couple of them, anyway. The shooting schedule had an early call for the ladies, and also an imposed curfew. That curfew required that they not leave the hotel after 9:00 pm and that they be in their rooms by 11:00 pm.

Of course, there are those people who must break a rule simply because it exists and, over the course of a few evenings, those of us who had to deal with this grew impatient. Combine this with a hundred complaints of various kinds and then came these two particular "Pets" who, after hearing about the rules and the reasons for them, figured that rules didn't apply to them, and tried to leave the hotel at 10:15 pm by walking out. Right in front of me! Shit, now I had to say something, because I was standing there with Pat Kennedy!

The girls were on the arm of a Major League Baseball player who was the boyfriend of one of the "Pets," and they were heading out to hit the town! I probably wouldn't have even noticed them, but Pat recognized the ball player from across the room. It was only as they approached that we saw the girls, and I had to say something. They were not happy. As I was explaining to "the boyfriend" why she couldn't leave the hotel, and he was pleading his case ("...but I'm staying at Caesar's and she's got a roommate here!"), Bob Guccione walked up, not to us exactly, but close enough to where he acknowledged us and the girls realized it's their jobs we're talking about. So, they dummied up and told the ballplayer goodnight. Then he told the girls he was going to go find someone else to play with who didn't have a curfew, which caused one girl to start crying hysterically! When it came to the "Pets," for the most part, it was like babysitting. With a couple of exceptions, these young ladies acted like spoiled brats, because they were. You'd think that a young man would find a bevy of sexy and beautiful women like this to be the big draw for this gig, but believe me, the view was best from a distance. I didn't touch one of 'em, didn't even try—no thanks! As I said, there were a couple of really nice ladies here, but for the most part, they were highly unprofessional. They were not trained actors, so at times it seemed to take forever to get things done. Unlike the professionals who were working with them, they were often unprepared or otherwise unready or unable to perform, and wouldn't you know it, they would be the ones to get impatient—unbelievable! Anyway, I asked the universe and the universe had answered!

The latter part of 1979 and most of 1980 found me working out of Las Vegas. I initially took up residence at the Aladdin for the Penthouse show, but then I moved to the Sands for the "New Faces of Country" show, and finally to the Tropicana for the "Jimmy Awards," a show whereby the stars of the Las Vegas Strip voted for "best of" categories. This was named in honor of Jimmy Durante, who had recently passed away. As I mentioned earlier, this period was busy morning to late night, but I loved it. Don't get me wrong, I had lots of time to see shows and dine and visit with the many friends and business associates who came to Vegas; it was just that these were long days. But I was twenty-five, so I could do long days! It amazed me how many of my friends and associates did come to Vegas! Prior to this, Vegas hadn't really been on my radar. Spending time there was really wonderful and eye opening.

Even though I wasn't entertaining at the time, at my core, I am an entertainer, and that was I how I was seeing and processing Las Vegas. And it was magical! Everything was so...BIG! The lights, the marquees, the buildings, the stages (the STAGES were huge). I was loving this electric atmosphere. One night, maybe the third or fourth night I was in town, I went to bed around 11:30, but was restless and couldn't sleep. After a while, I got dressed and headed downstairs to the main bar. It was there that I met Frank Gorshin, who, for my money, was the best impressionist of all. Frank and I formed a friendship that lasted until his passing. What an exceptional talent. Give him black coffee, chocolate cake and a cigarette after a house full of appreciative fans, and he was happy. He was a bit quirky, Frank was, but wonderful.

There was a period where he took to calling me in the middle of the night. My phone would ring at 2:00 am and it would be Frank. "Hey, Pete, I gotta tell you, my goddamn manager fucked me again!" And I'd interrupt and remind him that it was the MIDDLE OF THE GODDAMN NIGHT! We'd go on like this... He liked to kvetch, but he was a very entertaining kvetcher, but not at 2:00 am! Frank worked until two weeks before he died. He loved what he did. It showed. He was wonderful, a pain in the ass at times, but I count myself lucky to have gotten those late-night calls.

My time in Vegas was exciting. Working on the shows with huge stars, seeing shows around town, having backstage access, hanging out with my new friend Frank Gorshin, and doing all of this with the use of a limo, a beautiful suite, and being well-paid for this! I was in the lap of luxury! I worked hard, but the work was so wonderful that, if I could have, I would have paid for that job! I'm telling you it was almost indescribable! On top of all that, if I ever needed or wanted to go to Los Angeles, Pat Kennedy would make his private jet available if possible, and always have me picked up at Burbank Airport by a limo. He certainly was a class act.

I worked with and/or met so many stars that year that it seemed I had finally met them all. Not true, of course, but it sure felt that way. In the afternoon I was on a set with Wayne Newton and Liberace, and that evening at a party with Ken Norton (the World Heavyweight boxing champion) and singer Jim Stafford or Tina Turner. It seemed to go like this day in and out. Vegas does not stop. It was great. I felt that I was in the center of the entertainment universe. I, within the framework of the show and/or shows that I was involved with, was an important player, and although I was young, I was treated with respect.

Yet something was missing. I figured it was singing, performing. More accurately, it was the lack of singing and performing. I knew that sense of being unfulfilled wasn't due to my private life; I didn't have a relationship by choice. The hole I was feeling I'd felt for some time, all the time, really. Yet here and now it seemed quite strong. I really wanted to work here, in Vegas, at this level of professionalism and competence as a singer, as a performer. Yet the reality was that for better than two years, I had been making real money doing everything BUT singing! And, I started thinking that perhaps I had a problem. I wasn't sure what—depression, drugs, maybe both. What? I had actually cut way back on my drug use while I was in Vegas, but self-awareness was creeping in. With all the incredibly wonderful opportunities I had, with the money I was making and the famous and fabulous company I was keeping, was it really the singing that I was missing?

Tony Curtis, Bob Guccione, Robert Goulet, Professor Irwin Corey, Joan Rivers, Liberace, Wayne Newton, Sammy Davis Jr., Jimmy Dean, and Conway Twitty were some of the acts I worked with that year. Just being in town, I got to see or meet other wonderful performers or standouts like Tina Turner, Abba, Ken Norton, George Foreman, Jim Stafford, Pia Zadora, Ann-Margaret, George Burns, Peggy Lee, among others. And I'd not just see the show, but usually I was able to go backstage as well. I'd be introduced to the star and often was invited to hang out, unbelievably.

I was regarded as an executive, a show producer.

The reality was, I was an overpaid watchdog for Pat Kennedy's money. Come to think of it, I doubt I even got screen credit on any of the shows. But, it's who you know, and I was getting to know a lot of people. A lot of people in a lot of the right places. I had already learned the value of having such connections, yet the education I'd received in Hollywood seemed remedial compared to what was going on in this fast-moving town. In L.A., the guy who made mistakes or even cheated everyone might find himself down and out. You'd see those broken hustlers drinking the afternoons away in shitty bars. In Vegas, that same broken- down hustler disappeared into the desert. This was one tough town.

Chapter 6

ONLY IN HOLLYWOOD

Once again, I have gotten ahead of myself in telling this story. Try to understand that while Marty and I were developing and doing the medical videos deal with Pat Kennedy, things overlapped, such as what's coming. Not long after I left that crazy lady Ludmila's place, I went to work for Jack Millman, her ex-husband who had become my good friend. Jack had long planned that the two of us would team up together and he and I had, in the meantime, done many deals. The master recording tax shelter business had been very good to Jack. Jack and his brilliant fourth wife, Joy, built a tremendous business in a very short time, and because it was a highly specialized corner of the industry, they needed personnel with specific knowledge of this unique and new industry. And I was just the right guy. Jack and Joy hired me to license and "clear" music (meaning to get clear title to) that would in turn be licensed to a tax shelter company. It was pretty much the same thing I had done for Jackie Resources, Inc., except that in the beginning, no-name artists' recordings at nominal values were being used; now, we were licensing product featuring known artists, from Count Basie to Rod Stewart, for example, and for BIG MONEY! My market value because of whom and what I knew had climbed considerably, within a couple of years I went from being paid $200 per week by Jackie Resources to a salary of $70,000 per year, plus a car allowance and certain expenses! In the late '70's, this was a lot of money, plus I was still, almost as an impulse, putting deals together. On the money front, I had no problems.

The offices were in Jack and Joy's home, which was on Woods Drive in the Hollywood Hills. It was a sprawling, modern house that looked out over all of Hollywood and L.A. On a clear day, you could see the ocean from just north of Santa Monica looking north, and looking south to the hills above San Pedro, the Palos Verdes Peninsula. The views were fantastic. It was a magnificent Hollywood Hills home, complete with pool, Jacuzzi, steam room and wine cellar. What was once a game room was made into a combination editing studio and office for Jack and myself. Jack had his reel-to-reel tape machines where he would edit the music (he was a master at this) along one entire wall, and we each had our desks and there was a loveseat and two chairs for guests. Joy's office was a converted bedroom down the hall, and the office manager/bookkeeper was across the hall from her. The place was humming with activity. Nice. The house must've been at least 6,000 square feet, and required driving up a long, winding driveway that was lined with Italian cypress to reach a guarded gatehouse. Fancy stuff. Jack and Joy were doing very well. Hell, we were all doing very well.

Looking back, those were fun but crazy times. I do wish I'd saved a dime out of every dollar I made... man, do I! Even now, I talk to Jack most every day by phone. At age eighty-seven, he lives in Gainesville, Florida and is still sharp. Joy, God bless her, had passed away about five years earlier, but Jack keeps plugging away, still licensing music, supporting himself and even living alone. Jack is a real dynamo. A type "A" personality, he is always on the go. He has enough energy for three people! The eighteen months or so that I officially worked for the Millmans was a whirlwind of activity. I spent a lot of time out with clients, which meant I spent a lot of time with some wild characters!

A major client who we developed was a man named Al Biaggi. Al was a strange guy. He surrounded himself with an entourage of young gay men, mostly black and Hispanic, who would wait on him hand and foot. Al would pretend to be straight, insisting that that his "employees" were just that, employees, until he would get too drunk or stoned, which, not too long into our business relationship, became nearly all the time! Then he'd start swishing and lisping and pawing these boys like crazy! Al was something. But he had a huge catalog of master recordings. We met Al through a very successful and straight-faced producer named Mark Gordon. Mark Gordon originally was doing business with Jack, and one day, right after I started working there, Mark asked Jack and I to meet him at his office. At that meeting, Mark introduced us to his business partner, Al Biaggi. Mark explained that he was leaving that night for an extended trip to England—in order to avoid being served divorce papers. His wife, a member of the singing group, The Fifth Dimension, it seemed, wanted to tie up his assets, and by going overseas and funneling the business he did with Jack through Al, he'd gain an advantage.

It was clear from the beginning that Al was way left of center, so Jack, being no fool, set me up as the point man! I was in for some weird and rocky times with Al Biaggi, but when it came to his having knowledge of the music business and its players, he had it! In spite of his extreme nature, Al had hooks into all kinds of heavyweight musical acts, too. How and why, I wasn't really sure, but he did. Ann-Margaret and her dance troupe, Raw Satin, were close to him. Donna Summer, the disco queen, was also. I'd go to his office and end up hanging out with these people. It was wild! His office was actually next to his house, so I'd often find him there, hiding out with one or more of his "boys" or his clients. It seemed I was always chasing him for a tape or a contract. He wasn't very organized, and because he was stoned all the time, he was hard to deal with. Al's addiction was base cocaine. He liked to smoke it. His boys would prepare it for him and he'd sit and smoke like he was a king, a king that would drift in and out of reality and paranoia. He was a pain in the ass to deal with. He was always nice, but so disorganized. His saving grace was that he had the rights or could get them to some of the best recordings around. Picking up the tapes or the paperwork could sometimes be scary. Al's coke connection was one of L.A.'s biggest dealers and, as it later turned out, money launderers: Ron Waddy.

Mr. Waddy was a man who took to wearing fine silk suits under mohair overcoats, with a styling, big-brimmed felt hat, stovepipe pants, and small-heeled shoes. He had a beautiful, tall, thin black woman on each arm, and if he didn't roll up in his Rolls-Royce, it would be his Cadillac limo, complete with driver. Slow moving, the epitome of cool... that was Mr. Waddy. He was a little scary, too. Al was a friend of his, as well as a customer. Al, as I said earlier, smoked coke. He would also disappear sometimes for days. I found out that often, he would hole up at Mr. Waddy's.

Anyway, it seemed Al was always late with getting us something or the other, whether it was a contract or an appraisal or a tape. You see, we would buy or license it, and then we would sell or transfer it to someone else. When Al was late delivering something, it naturally held up our ability to complete our part of the transaction. I was chasing Al for a very large, important order and he finally agreed to meet. I showed up... but no Al. I got the runaround from his "entourage" and went back to the office, where Jack and I started calling everyone we knew who might have had a line on Al. We needed those tapes! Finally, after about six hours, word got to Al and he called me to say he had the tapes with him. He had to stop at Mr. Waddy's! Then, because he's now in no shape to drive, he asked me to come there, which, with Jack in a panic to get his hands on the overdue tapes, I had to do. Although I'd met Mr. Waddy many times at Al's, I'd never been to his house. So, Al gave me directions, and off I went to the other side of Mulholland Drive, to an armed, gated minimansion. I arrived after dark. The grounds were being patrolled by armed guards. I gave my name to the gate guard who nodded, and switched a gate lift, and in I went.

It was like entering a weird underground version of the Playboy mansion. The view towards San Fernando Valley as the early-evening lights started up was first class, but the only time I saw it was when I drove from the guard gate down the long driveway to the house. I was met at the door by one of the "guards," and then let into the house. Once inside the house, I saw that all the drapes were pulled, and the lights were dimmed. It took a minute for my eyes to adjust. I was then led into a huge step-down living room where, across the room, sitting in an overstuffed armchair was Al, sucking on a base pipe that was being lit by a beautiful black woman who knelt beside him. This woman was wearing what looked like a white, free- flowing, silk negligée, and with the soft backlighting, it was not leaving much to the imagination. As I stood and looked around the room, I saw Mr. Waddy sitting across from Al. He was being served a drink by another beautiful black woman wearing the same type of silky gown.

Then, Mr. Waddy signaled for me to come in and sit. Not a word has been spoken yet in this semi-dark room. I sat, and almost simultaneously a third beautiful black woman, clad the same as the first two, entered directly across from me. She crossed the room holding a silver tray in one hand, walking slow and seductively. She headed straight for me, stood for a moment in front of me, smiled, and then kneeled down to offer what was on her tray. There was a small crystal bowl containing base cocaine, and she had a fancy lighter and high-grade rum and q tips.

It's no secret, friends, that I liked cocaine, but, at this point in my rush to degradation, I had never smoked it. In fact, I'd heard enough bad stuff about basing coke that I was actually scared of it. Now here I was, in this very Twilight Zone–like experience, not knowing what to do, and still not a word had been spoken! I'd been there for maybe five minutes (which felt like FIVE HOURS 'cause it was so weird!), when I broke the silence. With this bizarre but strangely sexy scene going on, I had to turn down this "kind offer," get the tapes from Al, and get back to the office. I told them, "Sorry, guys, damn it, but I'm still working. You know, duty calls ..." Somehow I got out of there as gracefully as I could. Wild. I ended up chasing Al to Mr. Waddy's many times. Fortunately, Mr. Waddy trusted me, and I was always welcome— provided I called first.

Although people were not always partying and being waited on by the beautiful women at Mr. Waddy's (actually, it was rare), the ladies were always present and were always "in uniform" whenever I visited. That's just the way he liked it. He took good care of his ladies, and they, him. One time, I went there to pick up some tapes or something from Al. I didn't even turn off my car, as I planned to go to the door, be handed what I came for, and then leave. But as I got to the door, one of the guards told me to shut off my car and come in. Okay, I was in a hurry, but he had a gun, so, okay. As I was turning off my car, I noticed some activity back at the guard gate. A few guards had gathered and a couple more were approaching. Once inside, I was met with the same bizarre scene as always. I was greeted by one of the ladies of the house who led me down a hall to a bedroom, a side of the house that I'd not been to before. She took me to a bedroom where Al was resting on a king-sized bed, surrounded by oversized silk pillows and a couple of his boys. He was trying to be funny as he explained the reason I was brought inside and why the guards were on point; because he knew I wasn't going to like it. Mr. Waddy had just gone to war with a competitor, some other big-time drug dealer was trying to muscle in, and we were on lockdown!

I was stuck there until Mr. Waddy was sure it was safe to leave. And he was paranoid to begin with! This was about 4:30 in the afternoon. I was stuck there with Al, two of his boys, Mr. Waddy, a couple of Mr. W's associates, three ladies in white, and a bunch of guards until 5:30 the next morning. It was a very stressful night—Mr. Waddy nervously taking calls, getting information from outside. Al was splitting his time between the living room where he got high or the bedroom, where he disappeared with his fan club. Me, I was kinda left out. I didn't smoke coke, but I was supplied with all that I wanted to snort. Al was stoned out of his mind and Mr. Waddy had his hands full. The ladies in white, as lovely and seductive as they were, were strictly off-limits. Guards, kept coming in and out of the house, whispering to Mr. Waddy... It made for an eerie, stressful night. About 5:30am, I was told by Al that all was clear. I had coffee with Al and Mr. Waddy. As I gathered my things and headed for the door, Mr. Waddy stopped me. He quietly apologized for my inconvenience and said that he appreciated my attitude. At this point, one of the "ladies" showed up and handed him a small package, which he then gave to me, saying, "Thank you, man. Now you be careful going home with this."

I opened it when I got home. It was an ounce of really good cocaine. Really good. Mr. Waddy sure had style. About ten years later I read that he was arrested in Europe on narcotics and money-laundering charges.

"Only in Hollywood," as I'm so fond of saying.

So, working for Jack and Joy was truly an adventure. Jack was and is a wonderfully mad genius. The entire scene seemed to just keep going on, morning to night, Monday through Sunday. Business and personal lives intertwined. The lines were so blurred that most of the time, you couldn't see the lines, and if you did, somebody snorted them! Work hours were fluid. As long as I got the product and the associated paperwork in some sort of a timely fashion, all was good with the world.

I was still hanging around some with Marty Allred and Rick Marcelli, but more and more I spent time alone going to clubs, listening to, and I suppose, studying singers. I loved Carmen McRae. I saw her so often and requested the song "Star-Eyes" so often that she started calling me "Star-Eyes"! I enjoyed, really enjoyed all that the music scene in L.A. had to offer then. I was out nearly every night of the week, and there was great music everywhere; the Lighthouse, Concerts by the Sea, the Meridian Room, joints from the beach to the Valley.

But, really, I was running from that empty feeling again. What was I missing? Singing? Performing? I stayed very busy and was stoned a lot. But it seemed that was how most everyone in my world was (not Jack and Joy, by the way) so it seemed normal. That feeling of discontent was growing, however. I'm not sure how to describe it, the feeling had always, even to a very small degree, been there. A feeling of being an imposter... of being on thin ice... of... I thought singing might fill that hole, so I'd "sit in" and sing with a band whenever it was appropriate, which turned out to be as often as I'd like because I knew so many musicians around town. It was fun, but I was still "off." I couldn't figure it out. This feeling wasn't front and center, mind you. It was just under the surface—sometimes rising closer to the top, sometimes not, but more and more present.

Jack and Joy had become very successful, easily now being the top supplier of master recordings to the entire tax shelter industry. They had gotten to know not just the financial packagers who put the marketing programs together, but also the tax lawyers and specialists who interpreted the tax laws and structured the investment strategies. They had learned the workings of that industry so the next step in their evolution seemed obvious: why not form their own tax shelter company? The closer they got to making this a reality, the closer I got to the door. As I said earlier, I was feeling discontented and unfulfilled. Plus, the idea of being in the tax shelter business did not sit well with me; working at Jackie Resources had left a bad taste in my mouth, for sure!

As fate would have it, this was the time that Pat Kennedy called. I know it's confusing, but I was moving fast in those days. I had the system dialed in at the Millmans... I could earn my keep there and do my side deals. I remember picking up tapes for Jack as I drove the motor home to an appointment for Professional Video Services. I was hustling! Anyway, I wanted nothing to do with being part of a tax shelter deal, so, as hard as it was to turn down their kind and generous offer to continue our relationship of $75,000 per year, plus goodies, we did part friends and off to Las Vegas I went, with their blessings!

I would return to L.A. from Las Vegas with some regularity. Seeing as originally signed on to do a job that was to last just a few weeks, I had deals that were ongoing that needed attention, and an apartment in San Pedro with dead houseplants. Still, I had things going on in L.A. Pat understood this and accommodated me, flying me back whenever I needed to return. As my business with Pat Kennedy increased and became more centered in Vegas, along with my houseplants, my music licensing projects in L.A. were dying on the vine, and that was fine with me. I was feeling unsatisfied and more and more I was blaming the business of show business for my feeling this way. Truth is compared to performing or to being involved with productions like the ones I was involved with, music licensing was a total bore. Boring but lucrative, and I wasn't a complete fool, so once I left Jack and Joy's employ, I did retain a few "tax shelter," music licensing clients, a few of the clients who were mine originally. The time that I was working on the shows in Vegas kept me pretty busy, but because I had such good connections, I was able to acquire whatever master recordings my clients required.

Mind you, I was dealing with only three or four clients, but that still represented a lot of income. Times were good. If you ever saw the movie The Wolf of Wall Street, that's a bit overblown, but representative of the way the tax shelter guys lived. People like me those who were in supporting roles, didn't do too badly, either Personally, I didn't go in for fancy cars or boats. I did like nice clothes and watches and was happy to dress in fine suits and silk shirts.

But, as always, my real guilty pleasure was cocaine. But I was afraid to get busted in Vegas. While I was in Vegas I hardly got high. I was drinking at night, after work, but rarely getting high. It was a deliberate thing. A few days before I left for Vegas, I had dinner with Rick Marcelli at one of my favorite places, and his, Martoni's.

remember him telling me how he was quitting using coke by buying cashmere sweaters. He was wearing a beautiful dark blue cashmere sweater that he said cost $125, the same as a gram of coke at that time... so whenever he got the urge, he'd go to Beverly Hills and buy a new sweater instead of scoring. At that point, he said he had every color in V-necks, and was probably starting on cardigans the next day! Rick's a funny guy. That conversation stuck with me. I thought it made more sense to dress nice than be high, so when I went to Vegas, I went without drugs. And soon improved my wardrobe.

Friends from L.A. kept showing up with plenty of goodies, but all in all, I cleaned up my act. The irony, of course, is that of all the places in the world, this happened in "Sin City." But once I got back to L.A., man, did I ever slide...

Chapter 7

BACK TO REALITY

I got back to Los Angeles after nearly a year working on shows for Pat Kennedy. I almost actually bought a house in Vegas. I wasn't sure if I'd live there, full time, but more and more, I was liking what the city had to offer: shows of all kinds, lots of opportunities, and lots of action. Although the home prices were low and appealing compared to L.A., as were the bright lights and the fast pace of the town, it dawned on me that once my business with the shows I was involved with was concluded, I had few connections in this town. It only made sense to go home, so once we wrapped the "Jimmy Awards," I closed the production office at the Tropicana and flew back to Burbank. We still had a pick-up shot to do with Sammy Davis Jr., which we taped at his house in Beverly Hills. Once that was done, I cleaned up some odds and ends and satisfied my employment with Pat Kennedy.

Once again, I was left to make my way in the jungle of show business.

The energy difference between Los Angeles and Las Vegas was dramatic ...and I felt it immediately. I don't think I was back in town a day and a half before I called "Ed" and put myself through that crazy, live-wire tension-filled feeling that goes along with scoring—especially when it's been a while. Maybe it was being around Sammy, who was loaded out of his mind when we taped his segment the day before, that got me thinking about it again. Probably, it was just that feeling of insecurity creeping up again. Scoring a quarter ounce of coke HAD to help, right? While I was in Vegas I had kept my apartment in San Pedro. It was inexpensive and seeing as I didn't know when the gig was going to end, exactly, I kept it. My car, a nice BMW 528i, was a leftover bonus from my employ with the Millmans. In other words, my overhead was low. But I was back with the same problem: I lived an hour away from where my work was, and I didn't have an office. So, I rented an apartment in Hollywood, and rented office space from a record producer friend named Joe Saraceno. "Joey Big Head"! He had the biggest, squarest head I've ever seen. Wonderful, funny personality. We'd laugh by the hour. I never saw Joe make any money except for the licensing deals he did with me. He produced over 300 hits with the surf groups The Marketts, Surfaris and The Ventures, giving him royalties to last many lifetimes. He had written a song back when he was in college in upstate New York, which started a dance frenzy called "The Freeze" and had given him his start. He'd come to the office, make a call or two, go to coffee, come back around 10:30 am, at noon, go to lunch and eat till 1:00, back to the office, hang out till 2:00 or 3:00 and the OUT TO THE BAR! That was the routine. Joey Big Head—what a great guy! The office was on the 6500 block of Sunset Blvd. and kept me right in the middle of all the action. I was licensing music to a few hand-picked clients. These clients were high-dollar clients who focused on fewer transactions, but ones that required finer detail. I had taken on a "partner" of sorts a while back: my dear, brilliant friend Bob Carmer. Bob and I met through, of all people, Marty Allred. Bob was a brilliant attorney but was as unconventional as they came. Although he wore Brooks Brothers suits, he was anything but conservative. We became friends immediately. Bob saw that Marty was steering me in the wrong direction, and kind of took a big brother position with me—even to the point of protecting me legally by becoming my partner in all my deals, sometimes for as little as 5 percent; some deals as much as half. It depended on how much work he'd have to do. Bob saved my butt, for sure. My instincts told me not to stay with the Millmans when they wanted to become tax shelter packagers, as the subsequent legal challenges wiped out their financial gains, but Bob kept me from making a thousand bad decisions.

Bob looked like a short, squatty version of Tony Curtis. Brilliant man. While running his father-in-law's brokerage firm, Bob put himself through law school and passed the California State Bar all within three years, and, while he and his wife, Nina, juggled raising six small children! Did I mention that he was brilliant? He had no interest in practicing law, per se, but wanted the knowledge to assist in structuring his deals, primarily. He did get involved with other deals that he found worthy, and fortunately for me, he liked me, and we formed a loose, friendly partnership. Loose, because I don't remember ever having a written agreement between us. Sure, the deals we did with others were clearly laid out, but what went on between us was honored by a handshake.

Bob was a clean-living guy—always ate right: salad for lunch, light on meats, occasional glass of wine, no smoking or drugs. He didn't care what I did; he just seemed happy with keeping to his personal code. I asked him about this once, and he said that it was just his choice, but it turned out that it really may not have been. Not that he wanted to be a derelict, but the truth came out one evening when he called me from his hospital bed to update me on the terms of a deal, seeing as he was going to miss the meeting because he was in the hospital to get a HEART TRANSPLANT! He never told me about his heart problem! He had a system that produced cholesterol by the boatload and by the ripe old age of forty-seven, his arteries were jammed, and he was getting a new heart. It's true, for the last few months Bob had been huffing and puffing a bit more than usual, but this was so far off of my radar that when he told me, I just couldn't fathom it. I was so concerned for him, but also a bit pissed that he would keep this from me. One, because we were friends, and two, because we had a lot of business up in the air. I expressed my concern and he assured me that he had all the business up to date, and that I could pick everything up at his office. As far as his health, he put it in the hands of an excellent surgeon and God. And it turned out that the surgeon had good hands and God was paying attention. Bob came through the surgery with a strong new heart and within weeks we were back to business as usual, at a little slower pace, but I was very happy to have Bob back.

I was back to doing a bunch of crazy deals. Marty and I along with an "investment group," put together a re-release of Eddie Fisher's greatest hits. This was a challenge because by this time, Eddie Fisher was truly just a shadow of his former self. He was so damaged from his prior drug use that he could barely hold a conversation. His wife, a lovely Chinese woman, if I recall correctly, had to do everything for him—right down to taking him to the bathroom! His condition completely ruled out any promotional events that we had planned and nearly killed the deal, not that it was that big of a deal anyway. For me it was kind of cool, because Eddie Fisher was a part of history, and with my musical background, that made him important. But seeing him in in this condition, almost a walking zombie, was really sad.

Around the same time, I found a guy who had a warehouse full of "gravity flow" toilets that used less than a cup of water per flush, and I put him with a Saudi buyer who bought them all for his water-strapped country (that was a nice deal!). You see, I was moving and shaking with the rest of the deal makers. We were called "finders" for the obvious reason that we'd "find" whatever was required… and there was no limit to what might come along. The types of deals and people I got involved with covered a wide spectrum, from show business to real estate to personal loans, even to gravity flow toilets. The lesson of "working the room" that Marty taught me was my saving grace. I was always out meeting people with the primary intention of finding out what their needs were. If I could put them together with someone or something to satisfy that need, I'd pick up a commission or a percentage of the deal. That was how, with no visible means of support, I survived. Looking back, I have to wonder at the way I lived. I think I knew from that moment as a little kid when I told my mother that I wanted to be a singer, that I just wasn't going to fit into a "normal" routine. I just didn't see things the way others did… nine-to-five sounded like a prison sentence to me. My way of life, to my family and friends, looked like a life of insecurity and insanity. And they weren't entirely wrong!

There were times when it seemed nothing went right, and I wondered when and if the next deal would close, and sometimes I'd even start to question my decisions (maybe mom was right!). But overall, these were good times.

The "master recording tax shelter" business was still going strong. I had chosen to minimize my involvement in this industry by not staying on with Jack and Joy Millman as they built their empire. I also scaled down the number of clients that I would obtain (license) product for, as the business held no interest for me beyond the income that it generated, and the few hand- chosen clients generated plenty for me, with minimal brain damage. My time at Jackie Resources introduced me to the main players in this game, and for the most part, I had little in common with them. I was younger than virtually everyone else I dealt with, and many of the button-down suit types who came from the investment banking business found it hard to believe that a young, long-haired guy like me could deliver the goods. So, when I left Jackie Resources, I really thought I was out of the tax shelter business. Fate had another idea, because a few of those "suits" saw what I had done while I was with Jackie Resources and had sought me out to become a "buyer" for them. This is how I ended up with my core "tax shelter" clients.

My office with "Big Head" Joe Saraceno was, as stated earlier, on Sunset Boulevard, 6599 Sunset. Hooker central. The girls who worked the street would hang around outside the office building, standing on the corner, strolling along the sidewalks and do their best to attract customers driving by while also doing their best to avoid the cops. I would usually arrive at my office around 10:00 am, go to lunch around 1:00, and be back by 2:30 or so. Five o'clock was cocktail time at Martoni's for an hour or so, then back to the office till dinner. After dinner, usually at Martoni's, I'd often go back to the office to check on things. Martoni's was a block north of Sunset on Cahuenga and was a great place: great food, booze, and Lee the bartender could hook you up with anything you wanted (sniff sniff!). I would walk over from my office for cocktails and then again to dinner. I'd go there three or four days a week for both drinks and dinner because I'd see everyone I'd need to. Plus, lots of stars came in. One night I was at the bar and Robin Williams sat next to me. We talked, had a few, ended up having dinner, and then we hit the town in his limo. Great fun! But I never saw him again. Same thing happened with Chuck Barris of The Gong Show! Big fun. Connie Chung, the newscaster, was a regular there too; you get the idea. The place was wonderful, and everyone knew my name!

Martoni's and its owner, Sal Marino (no relation), were a Hollywood landmark. Anyway, being a fixture in the neighborhood, I got to know the "girls" on the street pretty well, not as a client, but more as a neighbor. Mostly, they seemed to have their own hours; there was the day shift and then the night shift. Initially, I'd walk by and of course one or more of them would sweetly suggest that we get more acquainted, and I'd explain that I was just leaving my office and was not interested, but as this scene repeated, I got to know a few of them, and we became friendly.

That progressed to the point that whenever the weather turned bad, or (as was much more common), the cops turned the heat up, a few of the girls would take refuge in my office. I remember nights where there were as many as six or eight ladies in my waiting room playing cards and drinking coffee, laughing and raising hell while they waited for the rain to stop or the cops to cool down. Crazy days. One night, as payback, the girls asked what I'd like, of course suggesting they show their appreciation in the ways they knew best. But I thought it would be fun if they took me to dinner—at Martoni's. You should have seen the look on everyone's faces as I walked in this fancy joint with a bunch of street girls. Priceless!!!!! Martoni's had private booths with curtains that could be pulled for privacy, and Sal, the owner, immediately stuffed us into one of those, out of sight of the "respectable" clientele! Once the drinks were flowing, and the curtain was closed, out came the coke and the party was on! Even Sal Marino joined us before long. We ended up closing the joint down that night. Sal locked the door after the last customers left and we kept eating, drinking, and partying nearly to dawn. Believe it or not, even though Sal tried to get a freebie or two, there was no sex going on. We just had a rip-roaring good time. Those girls appreciated my giving them a place to go when they needed it. They also liked being treated like ladies, and for that, they always thanked me.

Only in Hollywood!

Anyway, I'm finding myself settling into somewhat of a routine. I now have an apartment in Hollywood for my work, one in San Pedro for getaways, and my office in Hollywood. A typical weekday would start with my phone ringing at around 5:30 am, as my "tax shelter" clients were all based on the East Coast. I woke up to the phone, and after the first call would finish waking up with a couple of lines of coke and a cup of coffee. Between phone calls, I'd get showered and dressed and make my way to the office. I've already described my day, basically, but after dinner, I would often return to my office, or meet with friends or business associates. Singing was something that was now a rare occurrence. Even going to clubs to see my favorite singers didn't hold the same draw it once did. I was fairly consumed with this strange deal-making world I found myself in and had little time for other things. In other words, my days were long. Most days, I didn't get home until midnight. That phone was gonna ring again at the crack of dawn... It's a good thing I was young!

My primary "tax shelter" client was a gregarious Italian New Yorker I will refer to as Tony G. The name is being changed because, well, it is said the he is a "connected" man. He is also one of the funniest and nicest men I've ever known. But, in the spirit of privacy and safety (mine), I'm not using his real name. Tony G. was doing big business, and he's the one waking me up every morning! He had me looking for master recordings that were not only hard to find, but if found, were going to take a lot of negotiations, and a lot of money to procure because they were big-name product. He knew that I was also procuring product for a couple of other clients, and this bothered him. He felt that this essentially created internal competition, as I might be putting the same master up for the highest bid among my clients. Based on this theory, he made me an offer too good to turn down. He immediately took over all my expenses: office rent and associated costs, a secretary (which I'd never had before), my travel costs (he wanted me to meet in New York at least monthly), an expense account (Martoni's was expensive!), an office in his suite of offices in New York, and a FAT salary. As long as nothing got in the way of my work for Tony G., I was also free to do my own thing. Pretty good deal! Even Bob Carmer was impressed. So once again, I found myself with an angel, so to speak. For the position of secretary, I hired my lifelong friend, Wendy Mannett. Wendy and I had known each other since the second grade at good 'ol Holy Trinity Elementary School in San Pedro. We had become close friends in high school to the point that I had become almost a family member at the Mannett house. Wendy was like a sister to me, and I trusted her implicitly.

Business was getting serious now, and I was not the most disciplined person, so Wendy was a lifesaver. With Wendy in the office to handle the phones and paperwork, this freed me up, not only to pursue Tony G.'s agenda, but my own. Having her cover the basics almost felt like there were two of me, and I was able to make deals right and left! When I wasn't traveling to conventions all over the country with Tony G. representing the exceptional name value and quality of our master recordings, I was working the city of Los Angeles for all it had to offer. Time flew. Every two or three weeks I was in New York for a few days, then back to L.A. with stops in between: Chicago, Vegas, Newport, San Francisco, Seattle. Tony G. was getting his money's worth. While in L.A., I was still making the rounds, seeking product for Mr. G. and deals for me. Along the way, I got to know Lou Rawls. I was dealing with a production company in Inglewood, California, called Midas Touch Productions, and through them, I met Lou. Shortly after that first meeting, Marty Allred and I ran into Lou at a club, and wouldn't you know it, Marty knew Lou, too! For the next six months or so, I must have run in to Lou a dozen times—it was weird. Gas station, recording studio, restaurant, party... For a while, it seemed that everywhere I went, there he was. One night he joked, "Hey man, you following me?" Nice man. Always a kind word. What you see is what you got with Lou. Smooth and happy and so easy-going. And, what a voice. Even Sinatra said he had the best pipes in the business. One night, I introduced Lou to a songwriter friend of mine who I met through Joe Saraceno named George Mattolla. George wrote the beautiful ballad "Goodnight My Love," which Lou later recorded! Hey! Where's my finder's fee? This was a very busy time for me, and my breakneck schedule was taking its toll. Weekends, whenever I was in town, were being spent in semi-seclusion in San Pedro, mostly just to sleep. My cocaine use had increased, and I found that I needed R&R on the weekend to get through the week.

Jack and Joy Millman had become worried about me. We saw each other frequently. We did a little business still, but mostly whenever I could I'd stop by their house on Woods Drive to visit. They were not just my former employers, they were my friends, and they were concerned that I was burning the candle too hot and hard from both ends. They weren't wrong.

One side effect of being tired is slowed reflexes, and one afternoon slowed reflexes nearly killed me and landed me in the hospital. I was "managing" a wonderful dancer/choreographer named Jeri Bryan. I say "managing" because, although I did help her with her career, I really wasn't the most qualified. I did get her hooked up with a great photographer and got her portfolio dialed in. I arranged for her to choreograph a show at Magic Mountain, an amusement park about 20 miles north of Hollywood, but I really was winging it. Jeri had recently separated from her husband of a few years.

The morning of the opening of the Magic Mountain show, I met Jeri at Magic Mountain for a run-through, and her husband showed up. Thinking I was her boyfriend, he angrily pulled me aside to have a little "talk." I'd seen guys like him before and knew the kind of talk he had in mind involved very few words, so I quickly let him know that ours was strictly a business relationship! It took some convincing, and as soon as Jeri could break away, she joined us and assured him that this was true. He was embarrassed and apologetic. To make it up to me, he insisted on taking me out for a drink. I wasn't too interested; it wasn't even eleven in the morning. But it seemed like a good idea to get him out of there, so he and I walked to the parking lot. He wanted to drive, but his Fiat convertible was old and dirty so we, thankfully, took my shiny black BMW 528i. After a couple of hours listening to this heartsick sailor (did I mention that he was in the service?) tell me what a fuck-up he was, I couldn't wait to get away from this mope. I think I was feeling so sorry for myself for being trapped with this guy that I wasn't thinking about my drinking, and I must've been drinking too much. I didn't see that car run the red light.

I woke up in an ambulance. A car driven by an unlicensed and undocumented "alien" who was doing an estimated 65 miles per hour had run a red light and hit my car squarely in the driver's door, forcing my car through an intersection, up the curb, and against a light pole, trapping the drunken sailor on the passenger side. They told me that I drifted in and out of consciousness until I remember coming to in the ambulance. My passenger wasn't really hurt and was treated and released, the lucky bastard, but I was admitted to the local hospital with head and back injuries.

After a couple of days, I was transferred to San Pedro Hospital, where I stayed for eight more days— in traction! That's how they treated back injuries then: they'd hook weights to your feet and stretch you out! Well, so much for my shiny black BMW 528i, and so much for walking like a normal person. It felt like I had been bent in half; I looked like a u turn and couldn't stand up straight for a month. Totaled car, totaled back, and a head injury that would return to haunt me. But at least I found a way to get rid of that sailor! What a pain in the ass he was! By the way, I found out later that the ambulance drivers had put gum in my mouth to mask the smell of alcohol. According to them, it was clear what had happened. I was not the cause of the accident and they did not want the smell of alcohol to cloud the issue, so they took care of me. Nice guys and once again, someone, was watching over me. Can you imagine what would have happened if we had taken his little Fiat convertible? Jack Millman had a black 1978 Cadillac Sedan deVille with black leather that was like new that he was done with, so, mostly out of convenience, I bought it from him. Driving that big land yacht down Sunset Boulevard, I felt like a cross between a pimp and a gangster, but I gotta confess, I really came to like that big old boat! Since getting out of the hospital, my back always seemed to hurt after a long drive, like the one from my San Pedro apartment to my Hollywood office, so reluctantly, I decided to give up my getaway place in "Pedro." With everything so close and convenient, my activities during the week now carried straight into the weekends, and before long, I couldn't tell you if it was Tuesday or Thursday, Saturday or Sunday...because for the most part, when I was in town I was working the town, out seeing clients or trying to find some, on a constant loop it seemed—business and pleasure all rolled up into one. I don't mean to paint a dark picture here; sure, I was always "working," it seemed, but my "work" consisted of mingling with the rich and famous, in beautiful clubs, restaurants, resorts, recording studios. It wasn't drudgery.

There were great places that I frequented: Martoni's, of course; The Baked Potato; The Ginger Man, in Beverly Hills; The Polo Lounge at The Beverly Hills Hotel with good old Walter, the maitre'd. Once I had established a basic network of contacts, people like Marty Allred and Bob Carmer, for instance, I maintained a relatively steady stream of business opportunities. Combined with my "tax shelter" business plus what came to me directly, times were good.

But Jack and Joy Millman were worried about me. "You're working too hard. That's all you do!" Joy started in with me as soon as I arrived to go to out to dinner with them. "I've got a girl you've got to meet! She's just what you need! Nice Jewish girl... Jack and I are taking you two to dinner tonight." Joy had it all arranged. I was ambushed. Joy had her manicurist, Cindy Rosen, meet us at the restaurant, as a blind date. Joy thought that Cindy was a nice, clean-living Jewish girl from New York who would be good for me. You see, Jack and Joy were concerned that I was maybe using a bit more cocaine than recommended, and that the charms of a cute little clean-living Jewish girl would help to redeem me.

Only problem, that whole cute little, clean-living Jewish girl thing was an act. She was worse than me. She asked me if I had any coke on me almost as soon as we met! I slipped her my glass vile and she excused herself to go to the ladies room before we were even shown to our table! But she sure had Joy fooled! She was attractive, and that was enough for Jack, so he really didn't care. Well, Joy was right: Cindy and I had a lot in common (but not necessarily what she may have had in mind!).

Joy Millman, though not Jewish, had the heart and instincts of a very sweet, although at times naive, Jewish mother. Her instinct to "find me a nice girl" was her way of saying that she recognized that she saw something missing in me, missing in my life. She wasn't wrong. However, a girl, especially one with a bigger coke habit than mine, probably wasn't what she was really intending. What Joy was sensing wasn't my lack of having a mate, but my dissatisfaction with my life. I didn't understand why I felt unsure of myself, especially seeing as I'd accomplished so much and was doing so well. I didn't understand that constant feeling that laid just under the surface. Staying busy helped...real busy. The coke helped... helped me stay busy. Help me make friends, conversation. No, it wasn't as simple as being lonely. Don't really ever remember feeling lonely

Empty, not lonely.

At the time Joy introduced Cindy to me, I had just (at the suggestion of Bob Carmer) ended my exclusive relationship with Tony G. The writing was on the wall for the tax shelter industry. The I.R.S. was making lots of noise and threatening to close the loopholes that allowed this industry to exist. The best days were behind. I wasn't sorry. I don't mean to be or sound ungrateful, but for some reason, as much money as I made from it, as many places as I traveled to and as much fun as I had, I never felt part of that scene… always an outsider. It just felt like it had run its course. With the impending war between the I.R.S. and the tax shelter packagers looking like a certainty, Bob and I agreed that it was time to find new income streams. Point was, I had some extra time.

The blind date dinner turned out to be fun. Cindy was funny; cute, and very personable. We all had a good time that evening. Since it had already been established that Cindy and I both dabbled in the illegal powder, as we were leaving the restaurant, she asked if I wanted to go to her place to party some more. I told her that I had driven there with the Millmans and needed to pick my car up at their house. No problem, she'd drive, and we'd get my car later!

She lived on the fifth floor of nice high-rise in Hollywood. She showed me in the apartment, and then gave me a glass of white wine. I sat on a sofa and waited. She reappeared after five minutes or so, dressed in a silk pajama pant suit. She walked up and asked for all the coke I had, which was about two grams. She took it, went to the kitchen, and started to cook it. This was the first time I tried base cocaine. The first time I smoked it. The first time I danced with the devil, as I've heard it said.

I had some money and the ability to set my schedule. I had this coke to smoke and this girl to smoke it with. I had these underlying feelings of

97

nadequacy and dissatisfaction. All these ingredients added up to really bad combinations.

The next six months or so was and is a blur. My feelings of discontent seemed to go up in smoke, quite literally. Cindy and I spent most days behind pulled curtains (sunlight, I swear, is the drug user's enemy—it reveals too much) and the nights smoking the stuff. Forget about sex, when you're high on base, who cares about anything except staying high. Cindy quit her job, I gave up my apartment and moved in with her. Before I knew it, between the two of us, I was forking out more than $ 1,500 per week on coke! Every so often, I'd get mad and put all the pipes and paraphernalia in a trash bag and throw everything out. And Cindy would go out and buy more. This went on and on until finally, we agreed to dry out. We decided to move to Palm Springs. Her father had a beautiful home there and had offered to let us stay there while we looked for a place of our own. So off to the Springs we went.

Jack Rosen, Cindy's dad, was a stern, reserved man with more nervous ticks than a third base coach. He was in his late fifties, very successfully retired from the "fashion business" in New York. His father had been a mathematical genius nicknamed "Digits Rosen" by his boss, Benjamin "Bugsy" Siegel, the famous gangster. They named him "Digits" because he could keep all the numbers and the books in his head—a very valuable trait! Anyway, "Digits" and his wife had a son named Jack, and "Bugsy" and his wife had a daughter named Millicent. These two crazy kids grew up and got married and had a couple of kids of their own, Wendy and Cindy Rosen. Oy vey! Here I was, a nice Italian boy, smack-dab in the middle of what was left of the Jewish mob! Meyer Lansky was Cindy's "godfather," and would call to talk to her and Jack on Sundays. Occasionally, F.B.I. agents would be parked outside Jack's house, supposedly because of those calls. Jack thought it was funny, so every so often he'd send me out with coffee and donuts for them. Come to think of it, it was pretty funny. Sometimes, he'd send Freddie, his houseman, to do the same thing. To them, things like having the F.B.I. surveil them wasn't out of the norm. It had gone on literally all of Jack's life. As for me, I was more comfortable flying under the radar, if you know what I mean.

Jack, like most fathers in his position, I suppose, had a hard time warming up to me. I get it. I had no REAL job. I worked for myself, but I really didn't have a typical business. He felt like there was something "off" with me, and he did his best to keep me off-balance. I was polite and respectful to him, but I didn't play this game with him, and that, I could see, irritated him. Yet, he, too, did his best to be nice to me. This "coolness" went on between us for months. Before we moved to Palm Springs, he would visit from Palm Springs, always staying at the Beverly Wilshire Hotel in Beverly Hills. We'd go to dinner or the theatre, and he'd be polite but chilly toward me. This went on until one time when Cindy and I were visiting Jack in Palm Springs. We were out to dinner when up walked Lenny Garmisa, aka "Shirts," Mr. Sinatra's friend who I had done business with a while back. I stood to greet Lenny, and as he took my hand and said hello, he simultaneously saw Jack. It turned out that they were good friends! Jack asked how we knew each other. We told the story about how I drove down from L.A. and met with Lenny at his desert house. Then I told the Sinatra story.

"Oh, Sinatra?"

Now, Jack thought I was okay! He didn't love Sinatra, who had dated Jack's ex-wife, Susan, not too long before this (note: the Palm Springs area and the "in crowds" were very tightly knit, yet accessible) but if Lenny Garmisa had done business with me and liked me, and his daughter liked me, well, maybe I was alright after all. It was this switch in his attitude toward me that led to our staying in one wing of his beautiful Palm Springs home, and to be welcomed into his group of friends and associates.

The time was right to reinvent myself. I wanted, and thought that Cindy wanted also, to quit smoking coke. I wanted to find something exciting to do professionally. I wanted to leave Los Angeles. It looked as though the stars were aligning in favor of all of it. To relocate, we immediately had a beautiful country club home on a fairway, complete with houseman and our own private wing. I had a few bucks, so I looked at a couple of local, Palm Springs–based businesses. One was an upholstery shop, run by a true craftsman who needed someone to put in some cash, sell high-end work and expand the shop with more employees, etc. I was interested, so I set out to see how salable the product was. I was talking to Mary Sorrentino about reupholstering the bar seats at her famous Italian restaurant in north Palm Springs one afternoon around 3:00. No one was in the bar except us, and in walked Frank Sinatra.

Hellos all around. Mary fixed Mr. S. a drink, and he sat at the end of the bar, on HIS bar stool! That's right, they had a bar stool just for him. He sat quietly for a while as Mary and I talked at the other end of the room. Suddenly, he turned and said something like, "Petey, what are you doin' now?" So, I told him I was thinking about buying into this local business. He was in a reflective mood. He just nodded and went back to his drink. Anyway, Mary ordered new upholstery for all the bar stools!

Sorrentino's Italian Restaurant was classic Palm Springs. So, I wrote and delivered the order, but realized that this business wasn't for me. Before I knew it, I called my old friend "Joey Big Head," Joe Saraceno, rented an office from him again back at 6599 Sunset Blvd. in Hollywood, got a phone installed, and started splitting my time between L.A. and Palm Springs. At first, I would stay at the Beverly Wilshire (Jack would have me put the room on his account!). Soon after, I would stay at Cindy's mother's condo in Beverly Hills. Millicent had a wonderful two-bedroom, two-bath condo that Jack got her as part of the divorce. Millicent and Jack had a very friendly relationship. She often visited him in Palm Springs and was always a welcome guest in his home.

The fact is, they had known each other and been friends literally all of their lives. I don't know the particulars of their marriage, other than a couple of stories of Jack's infidelity, but from what I saw, Jack always treated Millicent well: lovingly and with dignity. And he paid for everything. And not just paid but paid for the best. Jack had class. He was old school.

While I was in L.A., I was back to my regular hustle, but now I was doing it without the aid of coke. Also, after "normal" working hours, I'd go back to Millicent's place for dinner, and to watch TV. I was getting so bored I thought I might die! What happened to my life? Down in the "Springs," Cindy was supposed to be looking for a house but claimed that her father was hampering her efforts. He was a very lonely man and enjoyed her company but come on!

This long-distance thing wasn't working very well because we didn't work very well—unless we were high. It just so happens that Jack was going to Vegas on business one particular weekend, and so Cindy suggested that I pick up something on my way out of L.A. and bring it to the desert house…

Oh, man—we were off to the races again! After that weekend, I was one lost soul. I realized that I didn't want to buy a house in Palm Springs with Cindy. I also realized that I couldn't stop smoking this shit and be around her. In my semi-paranoid state, I thought that Jack, with his supposed mob ties, might hurt me if I left his "little girl"! I was starting to dread going to Millicent's, not because of her—she was always great to me—but because it felt like I was being watched, like being there was a way to account for my whereabouts. Cindy wasn't so happy either. She was starting to take day trips to Laguna and Newport Beach, supposedly to see a girlfriend—only the girlfriend was a guy. While this going on, up in L.A., her dear friend, Tina Karl, daughter of shoe tycoon Harry Karl and stepdaughter of Debbie Reynolds, was making a play for me. I had no idea that Tina had eyes for me. One evening, I was picking up Tina at Debbie's house to go to dinner. We had a "friendly" dinner occasionally, so this was no big deal. I rang the bell, and her stepmom, Debbie Reynolds answered, and welcomed me in. Tina wasn't ready, so Debbie graciously took me into the library and poured us both a glass of wine. Well, I got to tell you, Debbie and I hit it off from the moment we said hello! We were on glass number two by the time Tina came in, and it must've been clear to Tina that I wasn't going anywhere. I stayed talking and drinking wine and laughing and hearing great show business stories till way after midnight. Tina was pissed, spending most of the night in a near-fetal position in a chair. I have to admit, I was a big Debbie Reynolds fan. Spending the evening hanging out with her in her home was wonderful, so Tina's pouting didn't put a damper on anything.

Debbie had recently opened her dance and rehearsal studios, DR Studios. Ann- Margaret and her dancers, Raw Satin, as well as Ben Vereen and other artists who I had some dealings with, rehearsed there, and I had recently visited them at her studios. This, along with some mutual friendly acquaintances, gave Debbie and me plenty of common fodder with which to spend what turned out to be one of the great nights of my life.

Only in Hollywood!

The "relationship" with Cindy was a sham. It's not that we didn't get along, because we did. It's just that we were more like brother and sister. We coexisted peacefully, generally speaking, as long as drugs weren't involved. We rarely had sex; I had little interest, sadly, at this point, and she had none —at least with me! I knew about her "friend" in Newport Beach, and it wasn't something that I was going to fight over. I just didn't care enough. Not about her... not about us... not about me... not about anything. I was just drifting. Drifting along with nice stuff: a few bucks, fancy friends, and places to go but just drifting. We kept this charade up for a couple of years, all told, I guess. At one point, we were lying horribly to ourselves and each other. During the week while I was in L.A., claiming to be drug free, I'd be chemically cooking coke in my car and smoking it while driving around L.A. all day and night long. Then I'd go on weekends to Palm Springs where we'd both spend a couple of days recovering. You see, Cindy was smoking her brains out during the week, too. And I was footing the bill! Once the account got to where she could no longer justify things, we both had a "come to Jesus" moment. We, for the umpteenth time, swore to give it up. Miraculously, I was somehow still maintaining a flow of business. I knew that Cindy enjoyed the lifestyle that both her father and I afforded her. She was wanting to buy a house with me, mostly because I had the money and she was tired of her sometimes overbearing father. She definitely liked the money I made.

Long after I gained my independence from Tony G., I, with the assistance of Bob Carmer, obtained the rights to three previously unreleased master recordings by a monster rock group. I'm not naming them because I don't want to dredge up the issues again. Anyway, I transferred these rights, one each to three different clients, one client being Tony G. Funny, his original reason for making a deal with me was to prevent this very scenario! Oh, well!

So, one day, these many months later, my partner and attorney, Bob Carmer, calls me with chilling news. Those very rare, wonderful, and expensive masters that we brokered turned out to be bogus! From a legal position, Bob told me, I was going to be okay. Seems he had done all the required due diligence and therefore "pass through liability" would go to those who sold to us and defrauded us. "So, you're telling me that we're in the clear, right?" I asked Bob. "Legally, we look good. But we might have a big problem. You sold one to Tony G. What do you think he might do to you when he finds out?" Bob was afraid that Tony G. might hurt me, or worse! Tony G. was a guy who I had made a lot of money with. He was a short, stocky Italian guy who was always quick with a hug and a smile and a handshake. Plus, he had the best belly laugh around. No, I told Bob, Tony G. would never do anything like that...Then Bob proceeded to tell me things about a man I thought I knew, things that scared the shit out of both of us.

Bob and I spent the next twelve days going between Los Angeles and New York City three times. In those twelve days, we structured a buyback of all three master recordings. I had to buy from all three clients. Couldn't do for one and not the rest. Bob and I were on a frantic pace. I knew that this was going to be life changing. My communication with Cindy was sparse and cryptic. I let her know that I was having some major problems, but I kept the conversations short and infrequent. I let her know that I'd fill her in when I got to the desert. Unfortunately, my assets and available cash did not cover the buyback. After paying everyone and everything, including all costs associated with closing my office in Hollywood, I was $70,000 short. Of all people, Tony G. offered to give me a "note" for the $70k. Bob Carmer hated the idea but saw no way to avoid it. Within maybe a month since Bob called and told me about the problem, I went from having a lot of everything, to having next to nothing, and being $70,000 in debt to an "alleged" mobster!

So, once back home in sunny Southern California, I settled up with Bob and Joe Saraceno. I had lunch at Martoni's and paid off my account. I filled my gas tank, leaving $1.27 in my pocket, and headed for Palm Springs. I felt like the world's biggest loser. When I got to the house in Palm Springs, Cindy met me at the front door. I had my carry-on luggage and briefcase, and with no offer of help, her mood became instantly obvious. After an uncomfortable moment of unloading my things, I was asked to explain my secretive and erratic behavior of the past couple of weeks. I laid out the entire tale, sharing every detail, including that the people who'd sold us the fake masters apparently had skipped the country and were holed up in Brazil, and explaining that I was, except for the money that we had in her account, the investments (in her name), my free and clear car (and let's not forget the $1.27 in CASH!), I was completely BROKE!

She sat, without moving, without blinking or breathing even for maybe twenty seconds. Then she very stoically looked at me straight in my eyes and said, "Let me help you pack."

Chapter 8

FALL FROM GRACE

Actually, Freddie, the most elegant and helpful, caring houseman in the world, did most of the packing. I remember being initially shocked, but after a few seconds, it dawned on me that this really was an honest and logical, albeit cold, conclusion. I processed this quickly and quietly. There was no arguing, no reason to bargain. I had mentioned what was "in her name" and she had responded. A lot was said in her single sentence. I decided to hang on to what little dignity I had, and without comment, stood and left the room to begin packing. Dear Freddie silently joined in, soon taking over, as he had amazing organizational skills. He didn't say a word until we heard Cindy leave. Then he said something like, "Mr. Peter, she give you too much trouble. You be better off. I love her daddy but she's a mean one. Now let's get you gone 'fore she come back." Freddie was the best. We loaded up my car with what we could. He told me he'd take care of everything else. We'd work it out once Jack got back from his business trip.

Again, in the space of just a few weeks, I went from having a lot of just about everything, to now having only a car full of my clothes, no office, no job, no phone, no home or place to stay, no bank account, and $70,000 in debt to a guy who might be kinda dangerous—and on top of everything, I wanted coke soooooo much. Nah, I don't think so—I've only got $1.27 in cash! This huge fall from grace happened so quickly. With my drug use of late, I hadn't exactly fostered any close relationships. Old friends I had let slide. My relationship with my family was strained and distant. And, as dysfunctional as my relationship was with Cindy, it had, at the very least, provided a roof over my head, plus a cook, and a houseman...you know, the basics. It was so tough roughing it! Just kidding, but it had given me some semblance of stability. Now, all of a sudden, I had nothing. NO THING!

After driving around for a while, I pulled to the side of the road to think. I had no idea what to do. How could I get started again? I needed money to find opportunities and find a place to work from in Los Angeles. I needed a place to stay, an apartment. I was pretty sure Joe Saraceno would set me up with office space and phones and such; sure, I was always straight with him, he'd understand what happened, he'd help out! Maybe Bob Carmer or Marty Allred would loan me $20,000 or $25,000, or the Millmans. My mind was going a mile a minute with possible people who could help.

But in the end, I couldn't bring myself to ask any of them. Here I was a mess. I knew it. I also knew that all my friends knew it, too. So why would they take a chance on me? I was in trouble, in a very real way, because I used too much coke. Sure, the cost of settling that business deal was unexpected and it was the right thing to do, but if I had been thinking clearly, I would have been able to better my position, been better able to absorb such a thing. Even I viewed myself as a bad risk. It was all so surreal. I was homeless. Just a heartbeat ago, I was living a lifestyle that was maybe not that of the richest of the rich, but I had all that I needed, and nearly anything that I wanted, within reason. My life was definitely charmed. I worked and dined and played with people of substance, sometimes even the rich and the famous. I guess this is what a pretty "charmed" life might look like. Right then, I felt anything but charmed. From top drawer and first class to dead broke and homeless. A true fall from grace, and from where I was sitting, it looked like a lot of bullshit to me. The more I thought about how cold Cindy was, the angrier I got! Money—I knew that the money counted, but I never thought it meant everything.

Again, I wasn't heartbroken, but I was hurt. How could she put me out knowing that I had nothing, no money, nowhere to go? As I sat there in the car full of my clothes, trying to fathom the depths of her callousness, I dubbed her the "Dragon Lady," which caused me to break into a much-needed laugh. "Dragon Lady": that's perfect. Here I was with $1.27 in my pocket, less than a half tank of gas, while she had plenty of cash in bank accounts (if she hadn't smoked it all up in the last couple of weeks), which I had put there. Something wasn't right, here. I was doing something wrong. Hell, I was doing everything wrong! I thought that I had that cushion to come back to, but, no. On top of everything else that had happened, Cindy Rosen turned into Dragon Lady and took what was left of my money. Could she really be that heartless? I sat and asked question after question, about where to go, what to do. Whom to borrow from. Would she really keep the money?

Finally, I had to do something about right now! I had made friends with a great guy named Frank Mastrantonio. Frank sold cars for a Honda dealership in Palm Springs, so I drove there hoping to find him. He wasn't there, but the receptionist called him at home for me. I told him briefly what was going on, and he told me to meet him. We met for dinner (he paid) and offered a temporary solution.

Frank and I met through Cindy's dad, Jack. Frank had sold Jack his "house car," which was a Honda. Jack also had a Rolls-Royce Silver Spur for more formal occasions...haha! Frank and I hit it off and had become golfing buddies. Frank was retired from Shilling, the spice company. He was well dressed and well spoken. He looked like Omar Sharif. Great guy. Anyway, after dinner, as we're having drinks, he slid over $500 so I could get by for a bit. He told me of a salesman he worked with, a retired colonel who had a room for rent. Then he told me that he could get me hired as a salesman at the dealership. Palm Springs in the 1980s was a pretty small town. You were either rich, or you were working in a service industry that served the needs of the rich. It was still a seasonal town. Once June rolled around, most of the moneyed residents were gone, off to their home bases, wherever that was that didn't get to 118 degrees Fahrenheit! And it was still small enough so that restaurants closed during the summer. This area was a paradise for eight months out of the year—a perfect playground for the rich and famous and those like me who were in their wake. But for the greater majority of the residents who worked in the service industries eight months of the year but lived there year-round, things could get hard.

And suddenly, I joined the greater majority!

I wasn't in a position to turn away Frank's generous loan offer; I needed cash. I wasn't in a position to turn down the job offer, either, but I did push it off. This was all too much to process. I really hadn't planned for a rainy day. I had "savings," or so I thought, in Cindy's name, which I had done to make her feel more "secure." Stupid me! There were also some investments, again, in her name. Although we did not have the romance of the century, I always felt that there was a core friendship, even my relationship with her father was really pretty tight; and her mother Millicent and I got along wonderfully. I never saw any of this coming. When I closed up shop in Hollywood, I paid everything and everyone off, at the behest Bob Carmer, in order to make a clean start. And with those "savings and investments," there would have been more than enough capital to restart. But I left myself completely unprotected. I got blindsided. I got hit hard. I felt beaten. Yet, I was stuck between begging for help or grabbing the only offer that was afforded me: selling cars in the hot sun for a monthly income that I hoped would be equal to what I used to make on any given day by noon.

I was a mess—and I still had a note for $70,000 held by a purported gangster that I had to pay!

I got a reasonable motel room for a few days. It gave me a phone number where I could be reached, and a place to decompress. The next morning, I called a few friends to leave my "temporary" phone number and to feel them out, to get a sense of whether I could ask them for help. I spoke with Jack Millman. He was pushing his latest brainchild, the Video Jukebox, which, by the way, is on display in the Smithsonian Museum in Washington, D.C. Jack had invented it and was structuring an international marketing program, plus running the tax shelter business that he and Joy had started. He was so enthusiastic and up that I just couldn't bring myself to change the mood and drop my bomb, so I called someone else, and couldn't tell them that I was busted out, either, and so it went. Until I called Frank Mastrantonio when I had finally decided to dig my way out and take the car sales job. You see, I couldn't, in good conscience, ask any of my friends for money. I needed to heal. I knew I could do without the coke. I knew it. I had resolved to rid myself of it before Dragon Lady gave me the boot, so at my core, I did not doubt that I could do without the coke. I truly did not doubt this. However, until I had shown this to be a reality, I also knew that I couldn't, in good conscience, go to my friends for money or help.

Sitting in that budget motel room, which was a far cry from the fancier lifestyle I had been enjoying, it didn't take me too long to size up my options. In spite of the heavy losses I'd recently incurred, if I looked hard enough, I was able to find the silver lining. Remember, I paid everyone off. I had no unsettled bills, except that damn note with Tony G. and the loan from Frank. I had no overhead, no rent, no home, sure but no rent! My car was paid for and I no longer had anyone around just taking from me. I liked that! I had no pressing obligations for once (good thing, because I had no way to meet them!). Of course, my first line of reasoning was to borrow enough money to get back to Hollywood and start putting people and things together again; being a finder. After all, that, and licensing music and all that show business deals lead to had been good to me. And I knew my way around town.

I was also just one of a hundred or more guys just like me in town, but now I was a busted-out one. And I'd seen how those guys were treated, how they were talked about. I never thought I could be busted out—never! But I had to face it. I was. For me to get back in the game I'd need seed money. Nobody does business with you if you're down and out. You never admit to hard times in that game, and my "friends" I thought would be better "friends" if I kept my problems to myself.

So, I decided to swallow my pride and take that job selling cars.

I rented that room from the retired colonel. We shared a two-bedroom, two-bath mobile home, nothing fancy, but very inexpensive. After a bit, the dealership gave me a "demo," which is a car to drive, so I sold my 1978 Cadillac and sent a couple of grand to Tony G. toward the note and put a few bucks away. Until then, I had only been able to send Tony G. $200 a month toward the note, but hey, I was doing what I could! I must admit, I had a good time during this nine-month period. Selling cars for me was like basket weaving. It was easy. I wasn't making much money. Hell, a good month was $2,000, $2,500. I don't need to tell you that that doesn't compare with the kind of money that used to flow. But working with Frank Mastrantonio was great. We'd golf and go to dinner often and we remained close friends until his death in 1998. I also became good friends with a wonderful comedian, Rex Meredith, that year. Frankie Ford, the singer who had the '50s hit "Sea Cruise," hosted a singing and/or comedy competition every Sunday evening called "The Gong Show" at a club in downtown Palm Springs called The Signature Room. It was a knock-off of the original T.V. show of the same name. Since selling cars was not nearly as stimulating as my previous activities, I soon found myself seeking out opportunities to sing.

I was sitting in with the local players, some I knew from L.A., such as Frankie Randall. Frankie was playing at a hotel in Palm Springs. It was great seeing Frankie. What a piano player! I loved Frankie Randall. I'd sit in with him, and some others around town. After I'd kicked off a bit of the rust from my voice, I went to Frankie Ford's "Gong Show" and signed up to compete. The place, although it was only 5:30 on Sunday afternoon, was standing room only. Frankie Ford was a great entertainer. He had the crowd totally engaged. He borrowed every "Gong Show" gag from Chuck Barris' TV show and pulled each gag off with the timing of the pro that he was. What fun! Acts of all kinds would perform; good acts, silly acts, and those in between. A trio of great local jazz musicians backed Frankie and all the singing competitors. A panel of "guest" judges sat at a front table and had access to the dreaded "gong," which they would, to the delight of the crowd, hit with a mallet to dismiss a horrible act. It was classic, and so much fun. The first time, I won first place: $50! The next week, I won first place again! The third week, a pretty young woman in a motorized wheelchair beat me. Her name was Robin. I won second prize. My second prize award was drinks, so we met up and decided to go out and to start seeing each other. The next week, we went to the "Gong Show" together, only to be accosted by an angry young man. It seems that this angry fellow was under the impression that Robin was his own true love and that I was treading where I should not tread! Well, here we are, in the middle of the extremely crowded "Gong Show," she's in her wheelchair bumping back and forth, ramming into Rex's leg as he's towering over me, hotly yelling at me while I ready myself to meet my maker. That's how I met Rex Meredith. Initially, he and I didn't hit it off so well. But later on, we became close pals and remain close to this day, even performing together.

Again, I wander. The point, I suppose, is that I was asking for a change, many changes, really. I wasn't satisfied creatively, personally, and certainly not spiritually. My ending the business relationships and activities of my recent past went along with ending many of my personal relationships and habits. I was not clear in my view of the changes that I was seeking. I did not expect the changes to be so radical. I did stop using cocaine. It wasn't that hard. I think I liked the idea of all that went with getting high more than I liked actually getting high: calling the dealer, rushing to get to the bank on time, that excited feeling as you weave through traffic, ten, now eight minutes away! THAT was the rush, the fun part. That first line was mighty good, though, but not worth it. I was done, and I was really alright with it. Yet it took time for my body and mind to adjust to living without it. I felt ... "off," yet determined to stay away from the shit. I further felt off balance from being so abruptly shown the street, and therefore simultaneously being broke, not homeless really, more like baseless and having to face the fact that it was all due to my poor judgment. My self-esteem was at an all-time low. My decision to disappear into the ranks of those in the service industry in Palm Springs would hopefully give me time to strengthen.

I needed to.

I needed to so badly in fact that, my exile from Hollywood was self-imposed because Tony G., upon receiving the extra note payment from the proceeds of my Cadillac sale, called and offered me a position with one of his companies. He kindly asked that I return to Hollywood and basically resume our previous business relationship, only this time, my salary would be $70,000. How about that—$70k! The same amount that I owed him! He didn't say a word about the note, but I was feeling the pressure. I wish I could convey what a fun and sweet guy Tony G. was. Even to think that this guy would hurt me or have someone else do it is beyond my comprehension, but Bob Carmer said he had reliable information that suggested otherwise, and I was remembering what Carmer told me as Tony G. made me laugh with some joke as he asked me to consider his offer. Tony G. and I had been pretty close. He knew I used coke. He didn't necessarily know that it was a problem, but he knew that I was a regular user. He himself didn't do drugs. He was a light drinker, smoked an occasional cigar. That's it. Knowing me as he did, I told him the truth. I thanked him but told him that I wasn't ready—that I was a mess.

I had just lost my money, my living situation, my livelihood, and I was detoxing. I felt I would do him a disservice. I recognized that I owed him, but that by taking the job, I'd be doing him wrong. He said that he respected that, and that he'd call me soon. He called every month, until five months later, he had me meet him at Los Angeles International Airport. He had a four- hour layover on his way to Hawaii and insisted that I meet him. I drove from the desert to L.A., dreading the meeting. Each of the last monthly phone calls had been more and more uncomfortable. I felt pressure because I still was only sending $200 per month and was certain that Tony G.'s diagnosis was that I was now ready to go to work again. The truth is, I wasn't. God knows I would have liked the money. But the money was only part of it. Along with the money comes the travel and the expense account, etc., etc. But I really wasn't ready. The entire two-hour drive to that meeting I kept running different scenarios in my head. I must have tried a hundred ways to tell him no. By the time I got there, I was a wreck!

But not him. Not Tony G.! He was his jovial, big-hugging, belly-laughing self. He was really happy to see me. I was sure of it. Carmer was wrong about this guy, I was thinking again as he's thanking me for sending the $200 per month, because he knows how little I'm making and what a hardship this is. He tells me he respects me. I really believe him. I'm still thinking Carmer, you're wrong! He inquired about my health, how I'm doing with, you know, without the drugs? We talk like the old friends that we are, and after a while, he asks if I'll take his offer. Will I come to work for him? He'll set me up in town with an office, a car, an apartment, the works. Plus, the salary. He says he has things working and he needs someone he can trust, someone like me. I thank him but tell him that nothing has changed. I'm still a mess, a bad investment, I told him.

He looked at me. The look was stern. He then reached down and pulled an envelope from his briefcase. As he opened it, I could see that it was my note for $70,000. He put the note on the table between us and said, "I'm gonna ask you once more." And although I was very nervous, I remember being struck by how kind his face was. How could I fear this man? I thought. My heart was in my throat as I shook my head, no. I told him that I still wasn't in any shape to do him justice, as much as I wished I could. He gave me a small, wry, knowing smile, picked up the note for $70,000, and TORE IT UP!

The initial response I felt was gratitude. I thanked him and hugged him as we headed our separate ways: Tony G. to the tropics of Hawaii for fun in the sun and me to the California desert playground of Palm Springs. Check that, to the hot desert where I worked selling cars.

As I walked through the airport back to the parking lot, it hit me. Sure, it was a great relief to be forgiven all that debt, but it also meant that my last connection to my former life, my last champion, had finally seen in me what I'd been telling him all this time: that I wasn't worth his time, energy, trust, and money.

When this realization became clear, I stopped dead in my tracks. It was as if the wind had been knocked out of me. All of a sudden, I seemed liked in just a few seconds I saw the last few months flash by, and I realized how much I'd let go, how far I'd run from anything that I related to cocaine or to Dragon Lady or to my life in Hollywood. I also saw that I had been fooling myself, because none of that was actually true. I let those things and people and places become excuses. It was that underlying feeling of insecurity and dissatisfaction that I was trying to outrun. Trying to hide from, not by overcoming my setbacks but by giving up and settling for selling cars and disappearing into the ranks of the "everyday Joe." Instead of challenging myself and tapping my abilities, I chose to play at a much lesser level. Bad choice, and the realization hit me like a ton of bricks. The drive back to the desert gave me time to think, to face the truth. It was time to pull myself up and to make my mark again. But where? How? I'd just had a huge weight lifted off of me to the tune of $70k, but I still didn't have any real cash, and I'd need cash to get back in the game in Hollywood. No without capital, that was out. Singing, as much as I loved it, was no way to solely support myself. Television production, although I'd been involved in a few shows, was really not for me. As the miles clicked off on the drive back, so did the ideas. Nothing was making sense, but knew that it was time for me to stop living this way. I had no idea how I was going to get back to my former income level and lifestyle, minus the drugs, but I made up my mind that I was going to. Why couldn't have felt this strongly just a couple of hours earlier and accepted Tony G.'s offer? I'll tell you why: 'cause I was still a mess, that's why! It was not fun being me at that time, but I did feel buoyed by my conviction to turn things around.

My social life in Palm Springs was a simple one. That was definitely by design. For the most part, I was keeping a low profile. I didn't frequent the restaurants or clubs that I did when I had been with the Dragon Lady. It's funny how, even in a relatively small town, that if you change your orbit, you start running into new people who are in that same orbit. Rarely did I run into people from my old life, and I wanted it that way. I was embarrassed. I had chosen to disappear into the crowd, so to speak, and I'd done a pretty damn good job of it. Mostly, I ran around with Frank Mastrantonio, as well as worked with him. Frank was also a great cook and loved to entertain. A mutual friend of ours, Stuart Rappaport, would most often join us. Frank would cook three or four nights a week, and we'd all meet somewhere for dinner on the other nights. Sometimes it would just be two of us, but usually, all three. We were a crew. Stuart was a successful investor who was working on a program with the owner of the dealership where Frank and I worked. As it turned out, Stuart and my paths had crossed in my "former life." We had met socially and had many friends in common. What a wonderful man. The three of us would laugh by the hour. We would go to the "Gong Show" together on Sundays, and soon into our little group came Robin, the young woman who took first place at the "Gong Show," as she and I became friends. And as fate would have it, Stuart started dating Robin's sister, Becky, and all of a sudden, Frank is cooking and setting the table for two more, and he loved it. It was like one big family. It really was fun. Stuart was generous with all of us. He'd treat us to nice dinners out, and even to a day trips sailing in Newport Harbor.

It was on that spring day in Newport Beach that Stuart told me about a new business model he had invested in. It was relatively inexpensive to start up, and within ten months, it showed a sizable profit! He wasn't trying to interest me; that wasn't his purpose. No, he was just THAT excited about this business. But he did get me interested. Very interested. The trip to Newport was also a "goodbye" trip in a way. Robin and Becky were leaving in a couple of weeks for Bellevue, Washington. That was home for them. They, like so many snowbirds, just came to Palm Springs for the winter and spring months. This was breaking Stuart up pretty good; he really liked Becky. As for Robin and me, well, we were just friends, really. And a good thing for me, too, because with summer coming and car sales looking bleak in 118-degree weather, Robin invited me to Bellevue for the summer. And Stuart had given me an idea. I was feeling stronger, too. Since my meeting with Tong G., my desire to get myself back to the income level I had recently enjoyed was outweighing my impulse to hide. The ability to get out of the desert for a few months was a Godsend. I needed a fresh perspective, plus, my pals were leaving for the summer: Frank was going to the San Francisco Bay Area, and Stuart, to Europe and New Mexico. We agreed to meet up again in the fall.

Chapter 9

A FRESH START

Bellevue, Washington, in the summer is as pretty a place as I've ever seen. Going to the beautiful Pacific Northwest was an ideal choice to spend the summer. My intention was to stay at Robin's for three to four months, as we had planned, then I would fly back to the desert if nothing better had come up. Armed with renewed self-confidence, I planned to take the summer to seek out ideas and opportunities to get me back in the swing of things. Staying at Robin's was less expensive than any other option I had by far—so much in fact, that it would allow me to take that entire time off from work. But that didn't pan out. I wasn't able to stay at Robin's. I mentioned earlier that she was confined to a wheelchair. Robin suffered from muscular dystrophy, and although she put on a good front publicly, privately, she suffered greatly. Sharing an apartment with someone who would have daily bouts of self-harming events was more than I was equipped to handle.

I had to go. Robin's other sister, Cindy, and her kids lived nearby and cared for her, thankfully, or I would have felt even worse than I did about leaving. And I felt bad, really bad, but I had to go. This poor woman was going crazy.

There was a Mexican restaurant, Garcia's, that had a bar where I'd escape Robin's outbursts. It was there that I met a very personable German man, complete with the heavy German accent named Rudy Kreybig. As I hit the bar for the third night in a row, Rudy and I laughed that I was also becoming a regular, just like him! So, for the third consecutive evening, we talked and drank and laughed, but this time, I had an angle in mind. By now I had decided to get out of Robin's place, as soon as I could, and by any means possible! I'm sorry, I know that the poor woman was seriously physically ill, but she'd throw things and yell and pull her own hair and hit and scratch herself, and on and on. It was horrible. I didn't know or understand then what I do now about mental illness; hell, the medical profession didn't! The poor woman. I wasn't unkind or impatient. I did get her sister Cindy involved as soon as anything started, but it was obvious to me that I had to go.

Rudy, my new friend, just happened to be the general manager of a high-brow Porsche Audi dealership right there in Bellevue.

Although I needed desperately to get out of my current living arrangement, I was loving being in the Pacific Northwest, and was considering staying for a while. I had nothing to go back to in Palm Springs or Hollywood, not at that point anyway. I wanted to go back, but not until I was on top again. And selling cars was NOT something that I wanted to do, but selling Porsches in Bellevue, well, that was a way for me to meet people with money, and people with money lived in Bellevue and drove Porsches, and that business idea that Stuart told me about was taking shape in my mind. So, I bought my new pal Rudy another drink.

I started working for Rudy the next day. The dealership was named Interlake Porsche Audi, and as fate and good luck and timing would have it, there happened to be an opening in the sales department, so Rudy gave me a shot. I took a bus to work for a week until I was given a "demo," and within two weeks of starting work, I moved out of Robin's place. Another salesman and his wife had a small ranch with plenty of rooms, so they rented me one. It was a twenty-minute drive out into the country, and it was completely different from anything I'd ever experienced. So, with everything being so new and different, I was feeling pretty good. Plus, I did okay at the dealership: the first month, I made around $4,500, which was plenty more than I made selling Hondas in the desert! The second month, I made around $6,000, and the third, I slipped back to the $4k range.

But during the time I was selling Porsches, with Stuart's help I had been structuring a business proposal. And I'd been meeting some guys in their thirties with money who liked to invest in new ventures. One such fine individual was Mr. Malcolm. He was, by all appearances, a true conservative. Brooks Brothers suits, wingtip shoes, straight posture—lots of starch to this guy. But as I got to know him, he loosened up a bit. I sold Mr. Malcolm a shiny new Porsche and, in the process, met and sold one to his friend, Mr. Peters, all the while finding out that they had been lifelong friends and were now business partners. They had a firm that invested in, among other things, new start-ups. Both of these fine gents shared a common trait among Porsche enthusiasts: an engineer's-type quest for knowledge and specifics when it came to the nuts and bolts of their new sports cars. Real pipe-smoking types.

Contrary to my basic personality, but because it was very much my job to know these details, I knew the answers to their sometimes-difficult questions, and they quickly grew to trust and like me. Had I not known my stuff to begin with, Mr. Malcolm would never have done business with me, let alone refer his friend and business partner. But he did, and the process of this took time. Enough time that the three of us got to know each other a bit. They asked about my background and were captured by how different my life had been from theirs. They had both come from stable homes and were raised in conservative, religious families. Both had attended the same university and had both married their high school sweethearts, had kids and settled down. Our paths sure were different! Upon finding that I'd enjoyed some higher degree of success than what my current job offered, they asked if I had greater aspirations.

WELL, FUNNY THAT YOU SHOULD ASK! I just so happened to have a business proposal all ready to go! This business that Stuart had invested in and suggested that I knock off was not a sexy deal, anything but. However, it looked like a moneymaker. Stuart was in the automotive service contract business and was very successful. When I met him, he was being groomed to become a new car dealer. He was forming a partnership to open a Honda dealership in Albuquerque, New Mexico, in addition to his other interests. He had recently invested in a boiler-room concept in Chicago to sell his service contracts, whereby automotive extended service contracts were sold over the phone. Basically, the dealerships supplied information about clients who bought cars but not extended service contracts to the "marketing company," which was the boiler room, the phone room. The "marketing company" would have a relationship with a service contract company (or many, usually by region), and would, on behalf of the dealership, call clients and offer them "special, one-time, too-good-to-refuse deals" to cover their brand-new, beautiful cars for years to come against certain mechanical failures.

The deal worked for Stuart and the start-up company in Chicago. The Chicago company had been successful selling office products by phone and applied the years of experience to make selling this new product line a success as well. Stuart wanted to help me get back on top. He knew this worked, if—and only if—a strict format and program is designed and followed. He helped me create a business proposal that included a consulting budget. In reality, the consulting agreement was more like buying a franchise. In return for the consulting fee, I got the Chicago company's playbook, A to Z. They had two years of staggering success, which made this deal very attractive. It wasn't show business, but Stuart kept steering me toward this. He'd say that "with a package like this," he was sure I could raise the money. Once I did, all I'd have to do is follow the formula. That's it. It works. And all he wanted was for me to do well. That was all. Stuart did not want a percentage or a fee, nothing. All he wanted was to help me. So, when Mr. Malcolm and Mr. Peters asked the timely question, I just happened to have a really professional business proposal ready to go. Thank you, Stuart!

It took a few months, but we made the deal. Northwest Dealer Telemarketing was born. With their investment capital and my sweat equity, I spent the next three years building that very unsexy business to a point that I could sell it. About six months into the deal, a consultant from the Chicago company, Larry, came to spend a week to make sure that we were on track. On his last day, we were having a late lunch at the restaurant in his hotel. We were the only ones there. It was about 2:30 in the afternoon and the place was empty. I was telling him that I was going to a Lou Rawls concert that night, and was hoping to see the singer, as we were old friends. He laughed because he didn't believe that I knew Lou, so I told him a couple of old "Lou" stories. He was bummed and said he wanted to stay another day. Larry, being from Chicago, was a big fan of Lou's and went on and on about how much he liked his music. Just then, from behind where Larry was sitting, in walked Lou Rawls. He stood alone in the doorway and looked around at the near-empty restaurant. So, I yelled, "Hey, Lou!" And Larry looked at me and said, "Yeah, right," not even looking up from his plate, until Lou, in his completely unmistakable voice, said, "Pete, is that you, baby?" I thought Larry was gonna drop it right there! You couldn't have planned this any better! It was wonderful. Larry's head whipped around so fast I bet he still has neck trouble! Well, Lou joined us for lunch, and Larry, although he hardly said ten words, had the lunch of his life while Lou and I caught up a bit.

I was missing show business like crazy, and seeing Lou brought this out, front and center! It's not like Lou and I were ever close friends. We were, for a short time, in each other's orbit. We had many friends and acquaintances in common, and shared a few showbusiness stories, much to Larry's delight. Lou was always so nice to me, and from what I saw, kind and generous to everyone who crossed his path. A true gentleman. I feel truly blessed to have known him, even the little bit that I did. But Larry! What a story Lou and I gave him to tell for the rest of his days—great stuff! And as always, Lou put on a fabulous show that night. Man, did I miss show business! My summer trip to the beautiful Pacific Northwest didn't turn out as planned. The three to four months I had originally planned to stay now looked somewhat permanent. I intended to return to Southern California to restart my life and career, but my friend and mentor, Stuart, pointed out that it might be easier to make a fresh start in a new environment. So, although inside I was resisting this, I realized that he was right. But having lunch with Lou and then being at his show, watching him work, hearing him sing and seeing the crowd respond to the magic that only happens in that world—that wonderful magical world of show business— made me, I don't know... homesick? That describes it as best as anything, I suppose. Not that I was homesick for a place, really, although I did miss L.A. and Palm Springs. No, more homesick for the action that comes with being IN show business. There is a special atmosphere that exists there. If you've ever been to a play or a concert or a show that's moved you, then you get what I'm saying. Magnify that by a lot, and that's what doing it feels like to me. I missed THAT! I missed working on creative projects with people who come from a place that only "show people" come from. Like the old song says, "There's no people like show people..."

Even though I hadn't performed for years, I was licensing music, brokering deals involving entertainment properties, working on television shows and hanging out with people in the business; my life had still been in and around show business. Until I started selling cars in Palm Springs. Even then, I was sitting in at clubs around town and having fun singing at the "Gong Show." And then I moved to Washington state and started this telemarketing business. This was as far from show business as I could imagine, and the scene was starting to close in on me. I wasn't made for civilian life. That, by the way, is what show biz folks called non-showbiz folks: civilians. And I just wasn't too well equipped to be one. I'd never been exposed to that kind of life, not really! Remember, I'd been working as a singer or producer since I was a kid. This was a whole new world to me, and one, I must admit, that I was not well suited for. And here I was, living the "civilian" life for some time, now. I was getting itchy feet, man, was I.

The business was doing alright. It wasn't growing at the rate that the Chicago company had during its first year, but we were on a respectable growth path. I discovered that I had second cousin living in Bellevue, Leonard, who, typical of the closeness of my family, I'd never met. I called him, introduced myself, and found that Leonard had just passed the state bar, but disillusioned with the prospect of actually being a lawyer, was unemployed. We met for drinks and I hired him on the spot. This was one of the best moves I'd ever made. Not only is he one of the nicest men on the planet, but he took control of the phone room and sales took off. And so, did I! I was having trouble keeping my eye on the prize. Here I was, playing businessman, having meetings every two weeks with Mr. Malcolm and Mr. Peters. Meetings to review the books (this was hard for me; I'd never done it before), to review sales, future projections, etc.! This, as basic as it was to them, to me was very foreign. I never went to college. Hell, I barely made it out of high school. I had run my business in Hollywood by the seat of my pants. I had good instincts, but when it came to budgets and projections and the like, forget it! This frustrated the hell out of my partners—so much so that they finally started coming in to help me with the reporting. But once Leonard was there, running the phone room and doing the reporting, that took so much off of my shoulders. It allowed me to concentrate on expanding the markets by increasing the number of service contract companies that we represented. That is where I shined. Dealing with the CEOs of national service contract companies was a natural for me. Wining and dining was right up my alley, and that was a now a big part of my job. Seems I had good training for this! And I couldn't wait to get out of there! As soon as Leonard got settled, I flew to L.A., where I met with a potential client, then drove to San Diego to meet with another possible client, MISCO. MISCO was run by a couple of young guys who were from the private banking business. They knew how to work hard, and party hard! Our meeting ended with glasses of very old scotch being poured to celebrate our "partnership." I had closed the deal. Our little telemarketing company in Bellevue, Washington, would now represent MISCO automobile dealerships throughout the country! This was a huge accomplishment—so big, in fact, that we had only a couple of months to hire and train enough salespeople to handle the flow of business that was coming our way. This one deal was effectively more than doubling our size. I may not have been the best at making projections and budgets, but after closing this deal, I was certainly a hero with my partners. In fact, within the next year, year two, we increased our volume by five times! We went from ten salespeople to fifty!

And in no time, I had found and was wooing a potential buyer. Jerry Wadsworth. A snake from Michigan who was a general agent for MISCO. I wouldn't trust this guy as far as I could throw him. He was a fast-talking, lying piece of crap and I immediately disliked him. He had an answer for everything. He was the biggest, the brightest, the most this and that. Just ask him! I couldn't stand this guy, but he LOVED the business, he had money, and I wanted OUT!

He had the state of Michigan as his territory and would supply my company with leads from his area. Through this relationship, he became familiar with my operation, and almost immediately showed interest in becoming actively involved. He flew out from Michigan to meet with me not two months into his involvement with us, and once he saw how effectively we operated, he wanted in— badly. I deliberately kept him away from my partners at first, who were unaware of my complete desire to rid myself of this "civilian" life and this soul-robbing business. But as his interest grew, I told him to structure an offer. My partners, by the way, shared my opinion of him.

He was a blowhard. None of us liked him or could tolerate spending time with this obnoxious bastard, but, as a client, he supplied a lot of leads, and now, as a potential buyer of our company, we owed it to ourselves to romance this pig at least enough to see if a deal could be made. Mr. Malcolm and Mr. Peters had no emotional attachment to the business. It was just business. They thought, kindly enough, that I had an emotional attachment to it, as they viewed it incorrectly as my "baby." It wasn't. It was a means to an end, and one I hoped was coming soon—very soon!

Once they knew that I was okay with selling, my business-savvy, college-educated partners tore into Jerry Wadsworth's proposal and tailored a deal that made sense to all parties. Except me! The terms of the deal left me in charge! No way! Looks like everyone missed the point: I want out! I want to get back to L.A., back to my roots, back to that crazy business known as SHOW BUSINESS! No way, sorry, no deal. I was beside myself. The success of this deal had little to do with me, and everything to do with my cousin Leonard. He was responsible for the day-to-day operations. He made the salespeople effective and successful. Okay, I had signed the big accounts, but only because the nuts and bolts of the business worked. That worked, not due to me, but because of the consulting agreement and business plan that I got (due to my dear friend Stuart) from the Chicago company to start with. And because Leonard implemented the plan. Keep Leonard, for Christ sakes! So, this master plan of mine was looking like it was going to backfire. And the funny part? It was because they thought that I was so valuable! Now that was funny—I had created a monster, and it was ME!

Along the way, I had had a few good teachers. One lesson learned was this: when caught up in a situation, take a step back, get some distance. See the situation from a different perspective, from the perspective of the other people in the deal. I started digging into Jerry's motives for buying the company. He was a man in his sixties, married, but separated with grown children who were older than his twenty-eight-year-old Hawaiian "girlfriend." Although very successful, he longed to get away from a nagging, soon-to-be-ex-wife and his unsupportive, very judgmental kids and former friends. To hear him describe his social position in Dearborn, Michigan, you'd think that he was a celebrity or the mayor, and one that the town had turned against because of his new lifestyle with the young and beautiful money-grabbing girlfriend. The more I learned about him, the more hope I felt that we could make a deal after all. You see, he wanted to get away from his square old life in Michigan as much as I wanted to leave my civilian life in Washington.

After negotiations that turned out stronger than I had anticipated, you bet we made a deal, and I was out! Well, mostly, out. I ended up with a consulting agreement with MISCO in San Diego. My end of the telemarketing company wasn't a lot, but enough to finance a new start back in L.A., which had been my plan, anyway. However, as word spread that I was out of the business in Bellevue, the guys who ran MISCO hit me with an idea: they wanted me to set up a phone room for them so that they could have an "in-house" marketing department. Seeing as the terms of the sales agreement with Mr. Wadsworth did not have a conflict with me doing this, I was able to set this up for them. They relocated me to San Diego, where I basically duplicated my former operation. In six or seven months I was done, but I liked San Diego.

Chapter 10

DOING THE "RIGHT THING"

I'm a guy who finds a way to fall in love with every place that I end up staying for a while. My hometown, San Pedro, although it has its rough spots, I still love. Hollywood and Beverly Hills, not so much, but the desert, Palm Springs, I loved it! Then the Bellevue/Seattle area— beautiful. So, you could say that San Diego got me. It wasn't the beaches. I love looking at them. That's it. They look great. But the sand's too sandy, too messy for me, and the Pacific is way too cold. Now in Hawaii or the Atlantic coast, anywhere that has warm water, then I like the ocean and don't mind the sand, somehow. No, it was the FEELING in San Diego. Laid back, easy. I don't know, it felt like everything was always coasting, gliding. Plus, being back in Southern California was heaven! As pretty and lush and green as the Pacific

131

Northwest was, I never got used to the gray skies and rainy days. San Diego was warm and mostly sunny, just the way I liked it. It was a time of little resistance.

I had rented a small, old house that was a block and a half from the famous Sunset Cliffs in the Ocean Beach neighborhood of San Diego. This little, iconic beach town was stuck in the '60s, with surfers and hippies so interchangeable that I couldn't tell the difference. The whole area back then was really charming. Everyone seemed to look after each other. The locals all knew each other, from the rich dudes to the surf bums. The best way can describe it is to say that the town had a "communal" feel.

This atmosphere recharged my creative juices. I started writing scripts and storylines for spec television productions with my dear friend Douglas Foxworthy. We developed a few show ideas and were shopping them around Hollywood. And I started licensing music again. Not for tax shelters anymore, but for discount racks and such. In the meantime, I was spending time in Palm Springs, sitting in and singing where I could, and trying to get a feel for who was who and what was what. And although I'd been a way for a while, it didn't take long to get reacquainted. During this time, thanks to my old pal Frankie Randall, I started to provide entertainment for some highbrow parties and functions in Palm Springs. Before long, I was producing shows for corporate clients and fundraisers, using big-name desert locals or visitors. But also, at this time, back in San Diego, I had a surprise production—I had been dating a woman who announced that she was pregnant. Wanting to be an honorable man, I followed the old school ways and asked, oh so nobly, for her hand in marriage.

She wanted nothing to do with show business. More to the point, she wanted me to have nothing to do with show business. I thought I was doing the right thing when I stopped my entertainment-related activities and started supporting us by selling BMWs. This way, I'd wear a tie to work every day and be home most nights for dinner and have a "normal" life. I really thought I was doing the right thing, but I was so wrong. Once again, I had been making a name for myself in the inner circles of the rich and famous of the Palm Springs elite, and I gave it up. This time, in part, to please a woman I really wasn't in love with. It's not that I didn't care for her, because I did, but it wasn't love. She was and is a nice woman, just not for me. And me, not for her.

I tried to adapt, once again, to civilian life. I worked hard and earned a promotion, becoming a manager in about six months. A year or so later, outwardly, I appeared to be fine. I went through the daily motions of kissing my wife and son, going to work, being the dutiful husband, father, and employee... but inside, I felt like I'd already passed the dying part and had re-emerged as a zombie. I loved my son. I guess that's what you call what I was feeling. It was all new to me. Whatever it is, the feeling is powerful—nothing I'd ever known, and I wasn't really sure what to do with it. But I loved it! Remember, I had little to draw on. My dad, when he was around, he wasn't around much, and when he took off for good, I was still pretty young, seven or eight, I think. So, there was that. And, I didn't want to leave my child fatherless, you know, like what happened with my sister and me. It was a mess, and I was miserable. His mother and I found less and less to agree on. It was then that Frank Mastrantonio, out in Palm Springs, put me on to an opportunity: to be a manager with a new dealership out in the desert.

The idea of moving back to the desert brought with it the false hope of new beginnings, so we all moved to the desert. Let me fast-forward here: an old tiger doesn't lose his stripes. I started back, sitting in, singing around town, and renewing old show business friendships. My wife wanted nothing to do with it, and yet that's all I wanted. One night, I was at Merv Griffin's hotel where Frankie Randall was playing in the lounge with his trio. After I sang a couple of songs, Sinatra, who was at a table at the back of the room called me over. We hadn't seen each other in about three years. He did the usual, asked about my father, asked what I was doing, etc. It was a great moment. It always was, seeing Frank Sinatra. It was Frank Sinatra, for Christ sakes! And once again, he remembered me—by name! So, I hurried home to tell the little lady that I ran into the "Chairman of the Board," and all I got was yelled at and told that I lying to her, making up grandiose stories.

Sadly, it was time to go. She didn't know or understand the world that I had come from, a world that, I think she found somewhat intimidating. She wasn't a bad woman, quite the opposite, and I wasn't a bad guy... We just weren't right for each other.

The next day, Frankie Randall called me because Sinatra wanted my father's phone number. When Mr. S. had asked about my dad the night before as he always did, this time I told him that my dad was dying. He gave me his condolences and said he thought my dad was a great guy, although as far as I knew, they hardly knew each other. Sinatra called my dad, and they spoke for a good five minutes, my father said. That was one of the nicest things anyone has ever done for me. That lifted the spirits of a man whose suffering I can't describe. Sinatra took away his pain, if only for a short while. Pretty nice thing for him to do, and I'll never forget it.

At the other side of my family life, as hard as I tried, I certainly wasn't cut out to be a civilian. Fathering was a role I had little preparation for, and once that role became part time, I really felt out of step with it. But I tried. When my son was with me, I took him everywhere From the time he was a toddler, he knew how to flow with things—he still does. He's always been one cool customer. Even now, we remain very close.

While I was working with BMW in San Diego, I had become friends with an automobile wholesaler named Mike Bennett. Many a day off was spent with Mike on a golf course followed by cocktails and dinner, and often, that devil powder, cocaine. We had a lot in common, and we had a lot of fun together. We became close friends. Mike was a Southern gentleman type, complete with a slow, easy drawl. Smart as a whip, good for his word and his handshake, Mike was a stand-up guy. My tenure at the dealership in the desert was short lived. I had obligations, and hustling show business deals took time. I needed something that turned cash, so I called Mike. We became partners in a little auto wholesale business. I'd buy the cars, trade-ins at the Palm Springs area dealerships, and he would transport them to San Diego for reconditioning and sale. Many of the cheaper cars, $300 to $1,000, I would keep at a dirt lot in Indio, California, that we rented for $75 per month. These cars would be sold to buyers from Mexico. It was like shooting fish in a barrel. I made friends at a high-volume Ford dealership in Indio, whereby I was buying all of their trade-ins. I was getting 50 or more cars a month for Mike and me from that one dealership, and I had four more. I would visit each dealership early every morning and negotiate on each car that I wanted, buying those that we agreed on. I was usually done with my workday by 11:00 am! Those were very good times! Good times. Oh, did I say that they were GOOD TIMES? Before too long I had the time, and the money, to license music again. And it took time to find the music and to place it, but the income from auto wholesale allowed it.

The music licensing put me in touch with such wonderfully creative people again.

And soon, I was spending my time with those like-minded souls, those who clapped on two and four, and they knew the names of obscure musicians and places that I knew. I was again among household names and the crowd that supports them. I grew up with this... these people... this business, and I had really missed it. Man, did I miss it!

So why did I try to be "normal" before? Why? Why did I run? How did I hide? Coke was one way; reinventing myself, I suppose, was another. Maybe.

Run... hide... run... hide—in plain sight. Well, it was good to be back, back with kindred spirits, back with people who looked at the world from a similar point of view as me; people who were show people. People who also hid and ran from themselves...

Just like me.

Chapter 11

THE START OF SOMETHING BIG

Maybe fifteen years back, maybe more, Jimmie Rodgers had me call his manager in order to license Jimmie's music. His manager was great guy named Bill Ficks. Well, Bill and I hit it off right from hello. He was classic, old school, show biz! He knew all the old show business stories of how that movie got made and that star got cast. He was amazing to talk to. And talk we did, at least twice a month for years. Through all of my changes, I'd call Bill and tell him how to find me. In those days, every time you moved, you needed a new phone number, and for a while there, I moved around a lot! But I always let Bill know what was going on. He was completely nonjudgmental. When I was out of show business, he would keep me up to date on what was happening, and Bill always seemed to know what was going on. Bill, besides working with Jimmie Rodgers, had his hand in all kinds of show business deals. As a matter of fact, it was Bill who sold the Six Million Dollar Man TV show to the network. Bill was wired in pretty well. He put me in touch with so many people and deals over the years, I can't begin to recall, and all he ever wanted was a phone call from me saying, "thanks."

That's it. (And the details of the meeting, of course.) He loved hearing the stories of how the meetings went and who said what to whom; he just ate up this stuff. He loved the details, a good story, a thank you, and knowing that he helped me. And for nearly twenty years our entire relationship was strictly over the phone. We never met in person. We talked all the time by phone, but never met. Wild, huh? Bill lived in the San Fernando Valley in a condo complex next door to a singer/actress whom I'd long admired, Barbara McNair. Barbara and I had met on a show I'd put together during my youth in L.A.

One day while talking by phone with Bill, he asked if I knew her. I told him of the show I put on featuring her and how much I liked her work and on and on, not knowing that I was on speaker phone and that she was listening. Well, I gushed on and on, even telling Bill how sexy I thought she was in the Playboy spread she'd done... I was a big fan! As to save me from total and complete embarrassment, I was interrupted by a woman's laughter, and then Bill telling me to say hello to— yup, you guessed it—Barbara McNair! Turned out that as neighbors they often shared coffee and meals at each other's homes. Fortunately, Barbara, always a classy lady, let me off the hook easily. Man was I embarrassed! Bill and Barbara had a good laugh, that's for sure! I bet Bill brought that up fifty times if he said it once, always with a big laugh like it had just happened... funny stuff!

Bill, now that I was back in the game known as show business, set out to hook me up with showbiz royalty who lived in Palm Springs. He called Ralph Young, the tall, deep-voiced half of the singing duo Sandler and Young, which headlined on the Las Vegas Strip for twenty-plus years. Ralph agreed to meet me, and we began a friendship that mostly took place over waffles at the Pancake House in Palm Springs. Ralph loved that place, plus it was only a few blocks from his house, and Ralph liked things close to home. Hell, he liked things close to his couch. I'm not saying that Ralph was lazy, he just liked moving slowly and staying in familiar territory. We would talk for hours over breakfast. I'd never get tired of hearing Ralph's stories. He never had a bad word to say about anyone. Ralph Young is truly one of the nicest men I've ever met.

After a couple of months of breakfast meetings, he invited me to a dinner party at his home. The first surprise of the evening was that Ralph lived two doors down from where I had lived with the Dragon Lady, and that his wife, Arleen, was my old neighbor! Secondly, at that dinner was one of my favorite comedians, Shecky Greene, and his wife, Marie, plus a retired agent from New York, Lenny Green, and his wife, Debbie, and another couple who I can't recall. Ralph introduced me as his friend, and that's all his "old friends" needed to hear. I was immediately "one of them." We spoke about common friends and acquaintances and projects, and by the time dinner was over, Lenny Green and I were making plans to get together socially. Before I knew it, I was being included in an old boys' network that money couldn't buy. I was having lunch with people like Jack Jones and Shecky Greene and Jerry Vale and golfing with Howard Keel. Keely Smith and her husband, Bobby Milano, were part of the group, as were Peter and Lauri Marshall. I was having a ball hanging out with these stars of yesteryear—man, the stories never ended, and with me being the youngster in the crowd, neither did the advice.

I had more Jewish mothers than I knew what to do with. My girlfriend at the time was a beautiful but soulless creature. Half the wives in the group were just like her and started pushing for us to get married. But it seemed like the other wives, the down-to-earth types, shied away from her. She wasn't very nice. She was just very pretty, and in that way, she fit in with this crowd.

But she wasn't nice. She could pretend, but once you spent some time around her, her true colors would ooze to the surface. As an example of this, when she was promoted to sales manager at the radio station where she had been top salesperson for the previous couple of years, the entire sales staff (save one), quit, and actually walked out, right on the spot! I had become pretty good friends with the station's owner, Paul, who immediately called to tell me what was happening. I was viewed (wrongly, I might add) as the only person who might calm her down and talk some sense into her, as she had shown the salespeople the door with some colorful remarks and was, as Paul put it, "out of control." He implored me to come immediately and go to lunch with them to diffuse the situation. That lunch resulted in my becoming a "part-time" salesperson for the station based on the condition that I could continue to run my business activities openly and as needed, even from my desk at the radio station. I had too much going on with music licensing, show and event promotion and all that that led to, to give it up to help them out, and they understood and agreed.

I'm happy to say that for the next two years, as a part timer, not only was I the station's top sales producer, but I also wrote most of the ad copy and voiced a majority of the commercials for the station's clients. Paul treated me so well. He would let me sign clients up as trade accounts.... There were restaurants where all I had to do was sign the check; high-end men's clothing stores fitting me with the best, for just a signature; golf courses and hotels, all on trade and at my disposal for helping Paul in his time of need. Paul was a stand-up guy. I never took advantage of his kindness. I worked hard to deliver and maintain his radio advertising clientele, and he generously showed his appreciation.

I did, however, sense a growing resentment from my "boss/girlfriend." My relationship with Paul, her supervisor, was all of a sudden becoming too "friendly." My having lunch with him, which was something we'd done at least once a month for a few years, was suddenly threatening to her. She wanted me to use my friendships with stars and producers to get her into show business, but she had no talent. I got her acting lessons with a great character actor and teacher I knew in L.A., Ernie Lively (Blake Lively's father). Peter Marshall would let her stay at his L.A. house, so she wouldn't have to drive back to the desert after class. Man was she bad. Even Ernie felt bad about taking her money. I remember one time he called to tell me although he didn't quite know how, how bad she was. Finally, not wanting to hurt my feelings (which he wouldn't have, 'cause I already knew!), he suggested that I attend a class with her. So, I did, and she lived up to her reputation! I was embarrassed for her. I must add that she was the type of person who thinks that they are the best at everything, even when they really suck! I'm sure you've met the type.

So here I am, obviously set with the task of delivering the news that the Oscar is not in her future. Hell, her teacher, my half-assed friend didn't even know how to tell her she sucked so bad that he didn't want her in class anymore. No, that was left to me. She wasn't happy to get the news! "What the fuck does he know?" She must've screamed rhetorical questions for the entire two-hour drive back to Palm Springs, and I don't think I said two words. What does he know? He was only one of the most respected actors and coaches in the business at that time. I think he knew a lot. Sorry, Ernie. I should never have introduced you to her. Hell, I'm sorry I met her, but more about that later. The deeper my social and business relationships became with these "famous" people, the more she wanted to be involved. But there was no place for her in my business. She was very successful as a media salesperson, but that was it. She had no place in my business world, and my social activities blended seamlessly with business, so this was becoming a problem. If she couldn't be a star, she wanted to live like one, hang out with them, dress like them... It was sad, really.

This group of aging stars, the men anyway, enjoyed her only talent, which was her movie star looks. But the much younger wives and girlfriends of these big-eyed, drooling gents generally didn't take too kindly to the competition and had no interest in her invitations to lunch or shopping. It didn't take long for her to figure out that the excuses were just deflections meant to limit her hurt feelings. They didn't work. She was hurt. Pissed, and she took it out on me! She came up with what she thought was a brilliant solution, one that would stop all the petty jealousy and catty feelings, one that would cement her position in Palm Springs society and get me a tax break to boot! You guessed it: get married! Well, that wasn't a sensible suggestion. Our relationship was a strange one, at best. Truth be told, I originally pursued her because she was deemed to be "way beyond my pay grade." She was the woman whom every man I knew hoped to date, but very few got to realize that "hope." Not only did I realize the "hope" of dating her, but about nine months into our relationship, she moved into my swingin' three-bedroom condo at the Palm Desert Tennis Club, and slowly started to erode all that had been normal life to me up to that point.

Gradually, I began to notice that my friends weren't coming around like they used to, and the social invitations I received were really business related. As I've said before, a lot of my personal and business life co-mingled, but at this point it seemed as if those friends I had who were not involved in business had all but faded away. She had that effect on people. She was (I'm not sure how to convey this) alluring and dangerous, cunning and manipulative, yet charming and sweet when needed. Bottom line here is that my friends were seeing things that I wasn't, at least initially. By the time that I was seeing clearly, my life was so entwined with hers that staying was, at least for the time being, the easiest choice.

Not all of the changes that she influenced were bad. Yet some-how I can only think of one: she got me to stop drinking. And at the time, I was drinking a lot, and that was just to keep the edge off of all of the coke I was doing (but I kept that part a secret). We'd eat out nightly, which had long been my practice since I don't cook. I would have three of four tumblers of Stoly's with a twist before dinner, maybe a glass or two of wine with dinner, and a Sambuca to sip after dinner. Plus, I was slipping off to the head to hit some coke to keep going. I was a mess once again. Anyway, one night, about two weeks after she had moved in, I woke up cold and naked on the living room couch with a screaming headache. Man, this was a sugar hangover, too much Sambuca! I remember how piercing the pain was as I sat up, wondering why I was there. Just then, she burst into the room, yelling how no one had EVER disrespected her that way! HER—who was so beautiful! How could I do this to her! She went on and on, and I thought my head was gonna split open. Yet I still didn't know what happened until finally I got a word in edgewise and asked, "What did I do?" This set her off again, making her even angrier! She couldn't believe that I didn't remember what went down the evening before (she didn't drink), causing me to explain, in detail, what I did remember.

My memory stopped with us finishing dinner at the restaurant, and upon interrogation plus a crash course on the effects of alcohol, she believed me and then explained why she was so angry. Seems we were getting romantic and I passed out cold, apparently at an inopportune time, leaving her feeling less than the most beautiful girl in the world that she fashioned herself to be. This led to an anger like I'd never seen. And the hangover didn't help. Without saying a word, she turned and walked out of the living room and back toward the bedrooms. I pulled on my clothes, which had been in a pile on the floor, and sat with eyes closed tight, head in hand, praying that the pounding in my brain would stop, and wishing that I could just go to sleep. Then I heard her walk into the kitchen and open the freezer. A moment later, she cleared her throat to get my attention. I looked up. When I did, I saw her standing before me, completely nude, her right arm stretched out to her side and in her right hand was my chilled bottle of vodka. She shifted her weight subtly, and with her left hand flipped her hair, still holding the vodka bottle outstretched. She said, purred, really, "Which would you rather have: me, or what's in this bottle?"

That was September 1991. The deal was that I not drink for two months. I had no problem not drinking, and I knew that I wouldn't. You see, I already knew where my skeletons were buried. I really only drank to take the edge off of the coke. I really never liked the taste or the effects of alcohol, especially the hangovers! And I was, once again, looking for a way and a reason to stop using coke, so perhaps this was divine intervention! Plus, my new live-in girlfriend had no aversion to my smoking pot, so should I feel edgy, I could light up a joint without comment. I could do this!

So, I mustered up all the strength and enthusiasm I had and exclaimed, "I'll take what's behind door number two!" and got up, took the bottle from her outstretched arm, and poured it into the sink.

Not only did I win the bet, but I still don't drink to this day. Oh, I might have an occasional glass of fine wine with dinner or a cold one on a hot summer day, but my annual alcohol consumption now might be two or three glasses of wine and maybe a beer or two. Yes, I said annual consumption. As for hard liquor, I can't even get past the smell. So, for that, I'll thank her. I took this "opportunity" to ease off on my coke use, and before long, I was down to using two substances: pot and nicotine, both of which I'd smoked since I was sixteen.

With my new-found "sobriety," I carried on with my busy life wearing many hats: media salesman, music licensor, show promoter/producer, auto wholesaler—whatever made a buck. A few months into this "relationship," we moved into a big house off of the second tee at the Indian Wells Country Club in Indian Wells. This was kinda cool for me because it was right on one of the courses where the Bob Hope Desert Classic was played, and where I had caddied so many years before. In a way, I felt that I had reached some level of accomplishment by living there, at a place where I had once been a caddy. It felt good. I couldn't wait for the tournament to come around. I was hoping to see my old caddy friends like Pete Bender, who had dubbed me "The Singing Caddy" seemingly light years ago, and my old pal Andy Martinez, whom I hadn't seen in many, many years. Both Pete Bender and Andy Martinez had made careers on the tour, and I was sure that they'd be there. Johnny Miller, now a commentator for NBC, surely would remember me from the days when Andy was his caddy, and we'd all have putting contests for millions of play dollars on the practice greens after the crowds had gone and the workdays were done. But when the tournament came to town, Andy wasn't working it, and neither was Pete Bender. I went to the television trailer to see Johnny Miller, and he gave me the bum's rush! I couldn't believe it! After all the time I'd spent with him and Andy on the road, and he claimed not to remember me. But when I said, "Johnny, I was Andy's best friend, The Singing Caddy, that you called 'The Devil'!" he showed recognition, yet still dismissed me.

Sure, he was busy getting ready for the day, but it wouldn't have hurt him to be nice. Oh, well. I guess he was still mad about that little incident in Atlanta all those years ago. Johnny was in contention on a very hot and humid Sunday afternoon. In those days on the PGA tour, things were much more relaxed. Security by today's standards hardly existed. I had finished caddying for my pro and had joined Andy and Johnny to cheer them on. I had just bought a Dr. Pepper at a snack bar and as I got to Andy and Johnny in the fairway (inside the ropes) they were discussing which club to use. Johnny was sweating profusely, suffering from the extreme heat and humidity, to the point where he was having trouble concentrating on his club selection. He saw me with the drink and nearly wrestled it from my hand. I told him not to, because it was a soda, but he grabbed it anyway, and took a huge gulp then swallow after swallow. Normally, this wouldn't be a big deal, but Johnny is a Mormon, and not accustomed to caffeine! He felt a temporary relief from the cold drink and resumed his club selection. I don't remember exactly which clubs were discussed, but I do remember being adamant with Andy and saying that he should take two clubs less, because Johnny had just dossed himself with caffeine, plus he was juiced by the fact the he was in contention with just a few holes to go. He flew the green with that shot and lost the tournament. And from that day on, he called me "The Devil." He recognized me alright that day in Indian Wells, but since he'd already been dismissive, and it had been so many years in the past, he let me go. I was pretty let down, to tell the truth. I had been so looking forward to reconnecting with my old caddy pals, and even Johnny Miller—maybe a dinner party for old time's sake. But, nothing. I was so bummed I didn't even watch the tournament at all that year.

However, in 1995, when Gerald Ford, George W. Bush, and President Bill Clinton joined Bob Hope at the Indian Wells Country Club for the five-some of the century (Scott Hoch was the pro in the group), I hosted a star-studded party of my own. My front door was across a narrow street from the second tee, not more than 100 feet, with good views from the front yard and driveway. My guests, hands full with food and drink, would wander from house to tee and back again reporting on who was coming in the next group. When it was announced that Andy Williams was due up next, Ralph Young and I elbowed our way up to the ropes so that Ralph could say hello to his old pal. Ralph, standing much taller than most of the crowd, stood out to where Andy Williams easily saw him and called to him as he came over to us. I hadn't seen Andy since that time I was with Nick Nolte at the Palm Restaurant many years before, and we really didn't part on good terms, but when Ralph said to Andy, after they embraced, "Hey, Andy, you know Peter, don't ya?" Andy looked at me, smiled, and said, "Yeah, I know Peter. So, what do you say? Let's bury the hatchet, huh?" and extended his hand. I smiled and shook his hand, and off he went, saying, "See ya later, Ralph." That was the last time I ever saw Andy.

Although I wish things had been different between Mr. Williams and me, I am glad that we at least ended on a good note. I do think that Ralph made that happen, just by being there. He was such an ambassador of goodwill, that his mere presence could bring the best out of people. I'm smiling just thinking about him.

Looking back, most of the '90s seem like I was running in place—a pretty nice place, mind you, but it's as if I was stuck on a plateau. I not only recognize that in hindsight, but I felt stuck at the time. Don't get me wrong. I loved hanging out with the elite of Palm Springs, the stars of yesteryear whom I really loved. The stories they told of that generation of music and movies, where Sinatra and Bennett and Basie and Bogart were kings, and the queens of stage and screen were treated like goddesses. I think I was born a generation too late. It was nice to do a little business with some of them now and then by licensing their music or promoting a show or concert. Being on a first-name basis with Keely Smith and Sinatra and Jack Jones, among others, was an honor to me. I had grown up listening to them and respecting them and their work, and now to associate with them was, in many ways, a dream.

Yet there was still that nagging sense of emptiness and of feeling unfulfilled. Without the "aid" of my old friend, that dastardly white powder that I used to love so much, and the fine wines and the vodkas with a twist, I was forced to see my world—and myself—without the filters those substances provided. It wasn't a pretty view.

My "pretty" girlfriend had, with each passing year, become more angry, spiteful, and hateful toward everyone and everything—including me. This caused her to be anything but beautiful in my eyes. And although my business activities were varied and profitable, nothing in that realm directly gave me a creative outlet. Socially, I was enjoying dinners out and golfing with my celebrity pals and my radio clients, my breakfasts with Ralph Young, and the house parties that happened nearly every weekend. Yet that nagging empty feeling, that shadow feeling, was prominent again. At first, I attributed it to the fact that my personal relationship was a wasteland; one that I was, shamefully, continuing because it was easier to. Then, I thought it was because I wasn't singing, at all. Although I hadn't sung professionally for a while now, I hadn't even sat in anywhere. I hadn't sung a note in years! This wasn't me. I suddenly realized that time was slipping away and I felt that, in spite of being surrounded daily by world-renown talent, I wasn't one of them, and that was what I had worked so hard to be, but I wasn't using my talent—my voice. I was so far away from my dreams it was crazy! I had drifted in directions that I could never have imagined. I was realizing that I missed singing and performing. My life had taken so many left turns, taken me so far off of my intended path. Yet, here I was, living a pretty nice lifestyle as far as anyone could see, one that I was too committed to, to return to performing. No time for that. But, damn, I missed it.

Realizing that I had put performing on a back burner for all the wrong reasons hit me right in the face! I allowed the woman I was living with to suppress my drive in this area, as it seemed to put a spotlight on her failure to ever rise as an actress; I also had allowed my business activities to serve as an excuse, throwing up a smokescreen of being too busy to pursue performing. Truth be known, I had lost my confidence in my ability to sing and I didn't want the brain damage that came with her being unhappy. I mentioned earlier that over time, she became more and more angry, dark, suspicious. It was as if she was coming undone. She was sick, mentally, but I didn't know it. She put on a good public face, but once we were home, she found no need to hide her hateful feelings toward everyone and everything (which, as I already mentioned, included me). Fortunately, her twenty-two-year-old daughter, who had been touring the country with a gymnastics troupe, got off the road and needed a place to stay, so she came to live with us for about a year. She not only provided a needed distraction, but she was a delightful person. She also brought, although too dim, a ray of light into what had become a rather dark environment.

With mother and daughter occupying each other's time, I decided to bolster my confidence and take a few voice lessons.

John Magaldi and his wife, Joan Steele, had just moved to Palm Springs from Los Angeles. I became friends with them when I worked with the Millmans in L.A. John is an excellent jazz saxophonist, and Joan, rest her soul, was a world-class jazz pianist and vocalist. Having never really studied voice before, I was captivated by the technique that Joan was introducing me to. My previous coaching sessions with Johnny Prophet and even those with Andy Williams never touched on these elements, and I was completely enthralled. However, when it came time to practice, I was often met with ridicule. From the hallway, my "girlfriend" would, in a mocking voice, try to duplicate the scales or whatever lesson I was doing. It was aggravating, to say the least. I would, of course, try to schedule my practice times when she was out of the house, but the prevalent attitude was one of condescension. And she made her feelings on the subject of my singing again known to anyone who would listen. Yet at this point, most people in our circle realized that something was wrong with her. Me, well, I knew how petty she could be. I figured this was some kind of sick payback for her not cutting it in Ernie Lively's acting class, and since I was the one who bore that message, this was one form of her revenge.

The constant belittling and mocking had its desired effect. After a few months of lessons with Joan Steele, I stopped. I'd heard enough. Sadly, in retrospect, I didn't leave the relationship then. For some unknown reason, I chose to stay. We worked together and entertained clients four or five nights a week. While doing this, we put on a good face and for all appearances, got along. However, once we got home, on a good night, she quietly went her way and I went mine, but all too often, she had a bone to pick. It didn't matter what it was about, she expected me to hear her out, and God help me if I didn't agree with her! On those nights, if the beef didn't start out about me, it usually ended up about me. I was an easy target. Thankfully, I had thick skin and selective hearing, and was way beyond giving a shit. But once in a while, she still found a way to get to me.

A few weeks before my fortieth birthday, she informed me that we were throwing a surprise party for a client/friend's fortieth birthday. Our house was a great party house. The living room was huge, with twenty-foot ceilings and one wall of sliding glass doors that led out to the pool and the patio and lawn. I didn't mind and took this as a good sign that my milestone birthday would also be treated as the big deal I had made it known that I thought it was. Well, our client/friend's party was a huge success, and with two weeks left until my birthday, I was filled with anticipation. Would she throw me a surprise party like this one? I hoped so. That really had been a great party and I spent the next couple of weeks thinking of how wonderful my party would be— who would come; would she hire my pals to play? I was really excited! The animosity between us did create some doubt, so the thought that maybe she'd just take me to lunch would get overruled by what a great opportunity this was for her to show what a great "girlfriend," or "party giver," or "important person" she was. Plus, she liked a good party, so I was pretty sure a "surprise" party was on the way.

My birthday was a bright, sunny, perfect winter day in the desert. I woke with an attitude filled with wonderful, happy anticipation. It was as if I forgot what was going on between us. I was oddly at peace with the world. I was expecting that she had reached out to my friends and clients to plan a party to celebrate this milestone! There would be great food and music, played by the best musicians in town. There would be close friends, old and new, some of them stars, household names, all of them wonderful people. Yeah, I cruised through the entire day with the same feeling and attitude that I woke up with. And I really had to hand it to her. She went through the day like it was just any other day. She didn't even say, "Happy Birthday"! Talk about playing it cool! Even everybody at the radio station was in on it; no one said anything. Proof positive that a surprise party was on! Okay, so I played along. Late afternoon arrived, and we left the station, separate cars, going home. I wondered why nobody had said anything; she must have had everyone in on the gag! So, we got home, and... nothing! No decorations, no people, no surprise. Okay. I figured she was going to take me out to dinner, and everyone would be at the restaurant, so I announced that I was going to shower. I came out showered and dressed, ready for a night out only to find her making herself a sandwich for dinner. I asked her what she was doing. Weren't we going out? She said no, why should we? I said because it's my fortieth birthday! She said, "Oh, I'm so sorry—I forgot!" I didn't believe her. I really didn't. I thought that she was putting me on, that she was still running the gag. Who could forget the fortieth birthday of their live-in boyfriend?

Even if we weren't exactly the couple of the year! Come on, really? But she really did. She forgot my landmark fortieth birthday! There I was, feeling more deflated and hurt and angry than I'd ever felt in my life. Yet what really was deflating was the knowledge that it was all false bluster. I wasn't going anywhere. I had, as sick as it was, just what I wanted. I had a life that truly was smoke and mirrors. Not that I was any great shakes, really, just living quite well on the edge of fame and fortune. From the outside, my life looked pretty good: attractive girlfriend, reasonably successful business, nice cars, clothes, house, stuff, fancy friends. But inside, behind closed doors, we didn't get along, no sex (or rarely, and, sadly, that was okay with me), I was happy staying busy with my work- related stuff, which included lots of meetings, lunches, and dinners and rounds of golf. I know... it was rough! Personally, I had no interest in a relationship, so having this "non" relationship at home had been, for the most part, working out. I told you it was sick. I allowed her to suppress my desire to sing. From early in the relationship, I let her take the lead—after all, she was "the boss." The problem was that, over time, she came to believe that she really was, and because it was easier to keep my mouth shut than to get into a fight, I'd keep my mouth shut. That set the tone of the relationship. As she grew sicker, she became more difficult to deal with, so I dealt less and less with her. But for her to care so little, to be so self-centered or tuned to such a different frequency as to miss my fortieth birthday?

I knew then that my self-esteem was gone. Why else would I be with this woman?

Lenny Green and I had become very close. Lenny was an old-time New York agent who truly fit the stereotype: good looking, a fast-talking, charming salesman type. Although he never discussed his age, he had to be in his late seventies, and he looked and moved like a healthy man of fifty-five. He had the most beautiful head of wavy, white hair and he didn't just walk, he bounced! What a character! Well, Lenny took to me like I was his long-lost son, and me to him. At first, like with Ralph Young, I'd meet him and enjoy his stories of the old days. Lenny was part owner of New York's famous jazz club, Basis Street East, back in the 1960s, and I'd get lost in the scrapbooks and stories for hours. Lenny was impressed with my knowledge of the business and its history, since I was so young! He had managed the clown Emmett Kelly, and upon his retirement, Lenny became Emmett Kelly Jr.'s manager. Being a very smart and clever man, Lenny, through the contractual arrangements with both father and son, owned the name and likeness rights, giving Lenny, the right to license pictures of the famous clown(s) on calendars, popcorn cans, greeting cards, damn near anything you can think of! Lenny made a fortune licensing Emmett Kelly and Emmett Kelly Jr. images—a fortune! By the time I came along, Emmett Kelly had long since passed away. His son, according to Lenny, wanted a similar deal to his father's, so Lenny happily agreed. Lenny told me that he put Jr. on a $4,000 per month contract that required him to do whatever live appearances Lenny booked. The only other requirement was that Jr. live near an international airport. He chose to live in Tombstone, Arizona, where, according to Lenny, he was the richest clown in that dusty old town.

You see, Lenny was knocking down, on good years, over a million bucks on that poor shmuck's image, while only paying him $48,000 per year! That right there should have tipped me off to Lenny's true character. His wife, Debbie, a nice Jewish girl half his age, never really took to me. From the start, she looked at me as competition. I knew it and so did she, and although she went through the motions with a smile, we both knew she'd just be much happier if I wasn't around. Lenny was bored, and he let her know it. She took this personally, although she probably needn't have. Her husband had led a high-energy life in show business, right in the heart of the action and in its heyday. Now, still with the physical energy and quick mind of a much younger man, he found himself surrounded by old men and women who had put themselves out to pasture! He was bored to death! It wasn't her fault. But here I came, a young man with knowledge of the business and an eagerness to do things. He called me his "legs." We'd come up with the ideas, and I'd have the "legs" to run around to get things done. That was the plan, and my being around got Lenny's juices flowing again. He was dreaming up ways for us to make a buck, promote a show, maybe bring a circus to Palm Springs! The ideas

154

were endless, and Debbie didn't like it. She wanted Lenny to relax, so they could enjoy themselves. They had the licensing business, that was enough. She wanted Lenny to herself and maybe to share with a few famous friends. Debbie was completely enthralled by anyone famous. She'd drop anything she was doing to accommodate any of Lenny's famous friends. A real phony, but Lenny liked her. She could drive at night he would say jokingly! He would yell at her, call her brutal names and just abuse the hell out of her verbally, and she would cower and take it like a scared little girl. It was pathetic. I'd get so mad at him and embarrassed for her that on many occasions, I'd leave.

Although I never cared much for Debbie, and I'm sure she never knew this, Lenny and I had many arguments about the way he treated her. He finally agreed not to treat her that way in my presence. He didn't keep that agreement, so I continued to walk out whenever he'd raise his voice, call her names, belittle her in front of me. He could be a real asshole. Anyway, we'd visit regularly, once a week or so to toss ideas around, get to know each other. For the most part, I tried to turn a blind eye to Lenny's faults. He was as much a lifeline to me as I was to him. I, too, in my own way, was bored, stuck in a rut, both personally and professionally, and Lenny was bringing exciting ideas and possibilities. I was eager to broaden my reach, and Lenny's seemingly unending pool of ideas and resources invigorated me. I hadn't felt this hopeful and alive in a long time. It looked like I had a new best buddy, and I liked it!

Friday mornings I'd meet my pal Ray Miller for a round of golf at Desert Falls Country Club. Ray was the director of golf there, and we had a standing tee time every week. Ray was a sweetheart. In all the years I played there and brought guests there, Ray would never let me pay for golf. Never! He was adamant about this. One time I did pay, and he chased me down in the parking lot to scold me about it! He was one of the nicest guys I've ever known. Well, this one Friday after we finished playing, I went to the restaurant for lunch and ran into Lenny Green.

Lenny was there for a "lunch bunch" meeting of show business types. Michael Dante, who has more than 100 movies to his credit as an actor, had arranged lunch at the club in a private room for people in "the business." Lenny figured I was there for that, but I wasn't, because I didn't know Michael Dante. Just then, Michael walked up and I was introduced. After a few words, Lenny took Michael by the elbow and led him out of my earshot, returned a moment later and invited me to lunch with, and possibly to become a member of, yes, "THE LUNCH BUNCH"! To be a member, you had to be in or a veteran of the business known as "show." You could have been an actor or an agent or a tech person—it didn't matter as long as your career was in show business. Michael Dante was hesitant to include me at first, because he didn't regard my selling radio advertising as being in the business. But Lenny came to my defense, telling him of my background as a singer, producer, and that I currently licensed music, etc., so the doors to the private back room were opened to me. Oh, what a thrill that was! The three of us were the first to arrive and sat at the large, rectangular table set for about fifteen people. Ray Miller came in to make sure everyone was taken care of, and when Michael saw that Ray and I were friends, he relaxed a bit... maybe I was okay after all. After a few minutes, in walked Shecky Greene, who I'd met through Ralph Young, followed by Jack Jones, who I'd met years before through Frankie Randall. I licensed some of Jack's music way back when, so now, it's looking to Michael like I just might fit in. There were maybe ten guys there for that first lunch.

I sat next to an older gent who was hunched over from a bad back. When he stood up, he was looking at his shoes! That's how bad it was! He wore a sailor's cap and a goatee and seemed to know everyone there. For the most part, I kept a low profile. Shecky was holding court and kept us in stitches throughout most of the lunch. At a lull in Shecky's "performance," this oddly bent man in the sailor's hat introduced himself to me. His name was Jack Rael. We started talking about music, as he was a music producer and artist manager, retired, and we quickly found common ground. He asked me what was my favorite live recording, and I told him that I had two: Sinatra, Live at the Sands, and Carmen McRae, The Great American Song-Book, Live at Donte's. He put down his coffee cup, very deliberately turned to me, looked me in my eyes, and said, "I produced that album for Carmen at Donte's." This was a wonderful coincidence—one that started a nice friendship between us. As well as Carmen's record producer, Jack Rael had been Patti Page's business partner and manager for fifty years or more, until she married her last husband, who broke up their successful partnership. My love for Carmen's work and my knowledge of her work both impressed him and warmed his heart, because he also loved Carmen, and missed her terribly. He laughed at the story of her always calling me "Star Eyes" whenever she'd see me at one of her shows because I'd requested it so often. So, I was in. Every Friday at 1:00 pm, if you were in "the business" and you were in the Palm Springs area, Desert Falls Country Club was the place.

Peter Marshall, Gavin McCloud, Bill Dana, Jack Jones, Jerry Vale, oh, the list of old and aging stars who became members of the Friday "Lunch Bunch" was both impressive and depressing. Impressive, because here I was, surrounded by some pretty strong players. Household names I had grown up admiring, watching on TV or listening to on the radio and on albums. Depressing, because these talented people, for the most part, had run their course. They showed up here, every Friday that they were in town, for friendship, to tell old show biz stories (that's what I loved), and to break the monotony of retirement. Although they were aging, they, for the most part, were fighting it all the way. They talked of the great times, the big shows, the times of their lives, the times that they missed so much. Because of the "stars" who came week after week, the lunches began to create a buzz among the residents and members of the club. The main restaurant was filling up with people hoping to get a picture or an autograph with or from a "Lunch Buncher."

And this gave Lenny an idea.

He wanted to get the "Lunch Bunch" guys with marquee value, like Jack Jones, Peter Marshall, and Jerry Vale, for example, to open a club! A little club where we could all hang out, and because we (the stars) would own it and hang out there, Lenny was sure that the civilians would come. He had proof! His proof was the success of the restaurant at the golf course on Friday afternoons! "Look at the all those country club ladies craning their necks to see who's having lunch," he'd say. We talked about this, and, talked some more. All the guys seemed to like the idea.

Finally, I was tasked with preparing a business proposal, which I did. After reviewing the preliminary findings, with the help of a realtor, I found a few possible locations for the club. Then I put together the detailed financial projections, marketing plans, the whole nine yards. Then we presented it to our most famous and moneyed "Lunch Bunch" pals. They hemmed and hawed for a month or so, no one able to come right out and actually say no. They had liked the idea before we asked them to put up some money, but now the tightwads were backing up! I was pretty annoyed. I had done a lot of work putting that business proposal together. I was having trouble letting go of the idea because I really did think it was a good one. And while Lenny may have had the initial idea, "Legs" had done all the heavy lifting, and I had given it a lot of effort. Having multiple "star" owners of a nightclub and having them visible in the place I still felt would work.

I was golfing with Howard Keel one day when, after listening to Howard lament about how his business here in "the States" had all but stopped (he was still very popular in the U.K.), an idea it hit me! These older stars didn't need or want a place to hang out. Hell, because of their celebrity, they were welcome most anywhere. No, what they wanted, no, NEEDED, was a place to work, to perform! Venues that used to book the likes of them had been drying up for years, leaving this incredible talent pool with fewer options and opportunities. My "Lunch Bunch" pals weren't in Palm Springs simply to retire, it's just that there wasn't that much work for them anymore. Sure, there were the community theatre gigs, PBS shows, and some overseas opportunities, but by and large, my pals were just as good at their craft as they always were and missed performing more than they would let on. No, they needed a place to work, to perform. I couldn't wait to finish that golf game with Howard so that I could get home and get to work tweaking the business proposal.

What I saw now was really going to be a success. I saw an upscale nightclub, not just owned and frequented by the "Stars of Palm Springs," but also featuring them as the performers! I was certain that this had been the missing element. This was what was lacking in our previous attempt. I went to work, writing a new proposal, reworking everything even before taking the new and improved idea to Lenny. Lenny flipped over the idea, agreeing with me that this had been the missing ingredient. Having learned my lesson after doing all the work on the original proposal for nothing, this time around, I clearly put myself in as the originator of the "concept," and wrote my position in as general partner, to which Lenny agreed, and agreed to support.

And that was the beginning of Basin Street West.

Chapter 12

BASIN STREET WEST

It took just over two years to get Basin Street West from concept to reality. That golf date with Howard Keel was on Christmas Day, 1996, and we opened the club on January 6, 1998. Sure enough, adding the element that made the club a venue where our "owners" could perform made all the difference! Still, it was no easy task to separate some of them from their money. And there were legal concerns as well. To address all the issues, we retained an old and respected law firm to draft the agreement, along with a respected Palm Springs accounting firm. This was no small business, and we were not approaching it as such. My financial projections were such that our annual gross income, adjusted for an eight-month season, would far exceed a million dollars, and the big-time accounting firm that we eventually hired backed this up. No, this was no small-time deal, and my position as general partner potentially had a lot of value. Our partners, for the most part, came out of the "Lunch Bunch," since the original idea was born and pitched there, as was the new and improved version. But don't get the idea that it was an easy sale, because it wasn't. Even after modifying the concept, and Lenny and me having gotten verbal agreements, guys backed out when it came time to sign the contract and write a check.

Other guys like Jack Real and Ralph Young were straight-up all along: they both said, and I quote, "Include me out!" They both said that they'd support the club but didn't want the headache of worrying about it! And they did both... supported the club, and as far as I could see, they never worried about it. As far as investors, we had the important ones, the ones with name value. Stars, household names signed on: Peter Marshall, of Hollywood Squares fame; Keely Smith, Jack Jones, Jerry Vale, Alex Trebek, Larry Gelbart, who wrote Tootsie and directed most of the TV series M.A.S.H., among others, and silent film star Buddy Rogers. These were pretty strong celebrity names to draw in the civilians, and, man, did it! But not without a lot of blood, sweat and toil. As I said, it took two years to get from idea to opening the doors in early January 1998. We had a "soft" opening with Buddy Greco as our first performer—not too shabby!

Opening night was bedlam. The room was set for 180 patrons, all with great sight lines to the stage. The room was almost perfect, as there were only two small posts, meaning that there were only two slightly bad seats in the house where you had to crane your head a bit. Really nearly perfect. The marketing had created a buzz throughout the Palm Springs area far beyond what our advertising budget could buy; everyone wanted in on our deal, now that it was happening. I was being interviewed on radio and TV and news shows, and Peter Marshall was, for much of this, making himself available, too. He and I were becoming pretty good pals. I was surprised by how much energy he was lending to the project. Prior to opening, I was the lead on getting the legal and accounting done, finding the property and negotiating the lease and designing the marketing plan.

Once we got open, I was to be the general manager, as well as the major shareholder. Lenny focused on getting the money together and lining up the proposed talent to book. Of course, both Lenny and I worked together so that we could cover each other if needed on any issue at any time, but we each had our primary duties. Peter Marshall, once on board, really got on board, working with Lenny to book talent, as well as doing TV, radio, and newspaper interviews both with and without me or Lenny. You couldn't buy the kind of coverage that we were getting in the media; it was wonderful! Everywhere you looked, there was an ad or an article or someone on TV talking about Basin Street West—it was something! Suddenly, I was being recognized and treated as if I was a star, too. It was all happening at warp speed. I was given the keys to the building at midnight on January 1, 1998, and that's when I met my construction crew—because we had less than a week to turn a Chinese restaurant into a top- notch nightclub. I had construction crews working twenty-four hours per day to complete this total makeover, which included installing a beautiful stage, complete with world-class sound and lighting. We were going to feature some of the finest talent the world had ever known, and I had less than a week to transform this building.

I did it! I say I did it because, except for pictures being taken when our sign was being installed and the occasional drop by to see how things were going, I didn't see much of my partners that week. Just as well, 'cause I was too busy to schmooze. It was time for me to take the reins and start managing, and let my partners enjoy their investment. The room was great, it looked wonderful and the sound was fantastic.

With barely any sleep that week, I somehow got the club ready for opening night.

Not being a restaurateur, I sought out and hired an experienced restaurant manager who took care of all things related to food service. I was charged with overseeing that, of course, but my experience had me taking care of advertising and promotion and helping Lenny with booking and related matters. Proper delegation of duties to well-qualified people we felt would produce desired results, but they didn't, at least not on opening night! We were slammed! Of course, we had anticipated this, so I had asked each partner to respond directly to me so that I could make sure they had a table for opening night, and I heard from everyone but Jack Jones. Sure enough, a half hour before Buddy Greco is to start, as the room is being filled past capacity by our over-accommodating maître d' and there was not a table to be had, my manager came to me in a huff. She said, "Jack Jones and his wife are at the bar and he's mad because we don't have a table for him"! To clarify, the bar was outside of the dining room/showroom. Peter Marshall happened to be talking with me when she delivered the news about Jack, and he graciously gave his front-row table to the Joneses; Peter and his wife, Laurie, squeezed in with some friends in the back of the room. This momentary panic provided Jack Jones with his favorite line that he used for a while, "I go to my own joint on opening night, and I can't get a table!" I like Jack Jones, and man, what a singer!

Opening night for Basin Street West was both a huge success as well as a lesson in humanity. We discovered that we had the wrong man as our maître d' because he couldn't say no, that we were sold out, and being oversold was a problem! A problem because it was nearly impossible to serve dinner and drinks; there was no room for the servers to walk! Thank God the fire department didn't come—they would have shut us down for sure! The showroom was set for 180 seats, and opening night we stuffed approximately 230 people in there. It was a madhouse! People complaining about the service, and getting cold food, it was a mess. Yet, in spite of those comments, the press covered us, saying things like these kinks will be worked out and they were. The press loved us, and so did the patrons, even with opening night follies. But not Peter Marshall.

The next morning, he called an emergency meeting at Lenny's house He yelled at me and berated me like I was a private in his personal army. He showed a side of himself that was so ugly that all I remember thinking was, "Oh, his poor wife, how does she live with this pig?" He was spitting mad. It was unbelievable. He was ranting how he won't let ME embarrass HIM with his friends because after all, we had the real Grand Opening in two weeks with Patti Page, and if I didn't have the problems fixed, he'd have my ass (whatever that meant). Anyway, I found out that day what Peter Marshall's true colors were, and that, because I wasn't a celebrity partner, he regarded me as someone "less than."

I told him two things in that meeting: one, that we would fix the problems, that's why we had the two weeks of "soft" opening, and two, that I thought he was acting like an ass and he should calm down. He didn't like that! He started yelling at me, threatening me with my "job" (he forgot that I was the majority shareholder as well as the GM), literally getting red in the face and spitting on himself! This egomaniac was unhinged! Lenny calmed him down, and Peter later apologized to me, but I never trusted him after that. As far as I'm concerned, he's a prick, talented, yes, but that doesn't give him the right to treat anyone like he treated me. He's another grand example of that old saying "Only the good die young!"

When our real opening night came with Patti Page, we were ready, as promised! Basin Street West was a phenomenon. Reservations were being taken for shows weeks in advance. I was working twelve hours per day, six days a week, and loving it! I had invested about two years towards this, and now it was a reality. I couldn't have been more proud as this truly was my baby. Everything associated with Basin Street West was top drawer. I had set up a trade deal with a new hotel, the Miramonte Hotel, in Indian Wells. In exchange for advertising, they gave us a one-bedroom suite each week to house our performer. This hotel was beautiful and elegant in every way. It allowed us to offer lavish accommodations that otherwise we could not afford. It was also at the front gate of Indian Wells Country Club, where I lived, so I was close should anything come up "after hours." Also, I had been approached by and I was beginning talks with Marcus Hotels, because this company was interested in putting as many as four Basin Street West clubs throughout their chain of hotels. Everywhere something was happening, and I was truly the happiest I'd been since I was a kid singer.

I had long since left the radio station and had settled into a semi-peaceful brother-sister-like relationship at home. Until the club really started to take off. My "housemate" was, as earlier stated, a frustrated actress and my becoming front-page news; getting TV, radio, and print interviews; being the Master of Ceremonies of each show at the club; and hanging out with celebrities and such... all together this was just too much for her fragile ego. So, she secretly plotted a way to be a part of it. One night she came to the club and announced our engagement, complete with a diamond ring! Well, mark my surprise! It was the first I'd heard of it! Not wanting to cause a scene, I quietly and sheepishly accepted the half-hearted congratulations from my partners and employees (they too knew that she was crazy), but once we got home, I let her know that there was no way that we were getting married— NO WAY! Then she informed me that she had charged the $17,000 diamond ring to my account at my friend's jewelry store! Now I was really hot! The next morning, I called and straightened that out on my way to the club.

Around noon, my recently former fiancé called to tell me to come to the house immediately, or all of my clothes would be cut up and painted and thrown on the lawn or in the pool—I had thirty minutes! I was extremely busy, but after many crazy, threatening calls, around four hours later I went home. Lainie Kazan was the performer that week and, as usual, we were sold out, and this was Saturday night. The last thing I needed was a front-row seat to a psychic meltdown, but there was no avoiding it. Plus, I needed to clean up and put on a suit for the night. I opened the front door and found her standing in the living room in a fighting position over a large pile of what used to be my entire wardrobe! She had in her hands a 2x2 stick, which was about 4 feet long with nails on the end of it. I had used this as a tool to hang things that were too high for me to reach. Once I crossed the threshold with the door closed behind me, she charged—striking me with this stick, and with her free hand, scratching my neck and face, pulling my hair, catching me completely by surprise. She was totally out of control. I had never hit a woman, and now, with that drilled so deeply into me that I shouldn't, all I did was my best to fend her off. Finally, I was able to push her over the pile of torn and painted suits and ties and sport coats and dress shoes, and escape with just the clothes on my back. The car I had been driving was hers, so I threw down the keys on my way out. My clothes were torn, and my face and neck were deeply scratched and bleeding, and I didn't know what to do or where to go. I started walking around the golf course until I realized that I had to do something; I had a dinner show starting in a few hours! Once my adrenaline dropped to a level that let me think, I walked to the Miramonte Hotel, and in all my glory strolled through the lush lobby to the concierge desk and asked for the sales manager. Of course, in my bleeding and disheveled condition, I was met with suspicion. I looked like a homeless guy (oh, I guess I had just become one), and one who had just took a beating at that, and certainly not like someone who belonged in this elegant hotel!

The young lady took my name and in hushed tones called the manager, who immediately recognized my name and hurried to the lobby to meet me. You see, although I'd had a trade deal for my performers to stay here, I did the deal all by phone and fax. I had never actually met the hotel personnel, until now—in all my glory. Imagine my embarrassment. Here I was, a half-assed celebrity in my own right, still shaking and bleeding, clothes torn, and hair messed up, finally meeting face to face and having to ask for a favor. And during the scuffle, my wallet had fallen out, so I had nothing: no ID, no money, nothing. The hotel manager's name was Susan, and as soon as she saw me, she mercifully took me to a private office out of the sight of the hotel guests. Since I had discovered that my wallet was gone, I now, after answering her questions about whether I needed an ambulance, etc., simply asked if I could use a phone and have a place to wait until I figured this out. She said I could wait upstairs—in a one-bedroom suite! She had a beautiful suite prepared for me, telling me not to worry about a thing. Once I was settled in the room, a bellhop arrived with a tray of food and drinks, and another tray of every kind of toiletries one could imagine. I was being treated like a king. And all on the house! Man was that nice! I got on the phone and called my pal Frank Grosso. Frank owed Desmond's Men's Store in Palm Springs, and when he heard what had happened, he told me not to worry. He'd pick me up in the morning and set me up with a wardrobe. I then called Lenny and told him about the situation, and that I wouldn't be at the club that night. The next morning, Frank Grosso took me to his store, outfitted me with four new suits, two sport coats, some slacks, shirts, ties, socks, underwear, three pairs of shoes—the whole nine yards. He had his tailor fit me on the spot, so I'd be ready for the show on Tuesday! The bill came to more than $4,000. He never gave it to me, would never send it, would never let me see it, told me to forget it! This was one special man. Thanks again, Frank. I know that you can hear me in heaven.

So, in the space of a day and a half, after going through that violent breakup, I realized what a relief it was not to be with her. Although for years, and I know this sounds strange, we had settled into weird existence, like we were mostly numb to each other (at home, anyway). Now that I was out, I clearly saw what a negative draw she was on everything that she touched. And as soon as I left, I was met with overwhelming kindness and generosity. I took this as a sign!

Within a week I had leased a new car and a new apartment and felt as if I had a new lease on life itself! The crew at the club had a tradition of taking out the "star of the week" on Sunday night after the last show. I had never gone before, so after much persuading, I joined them for Dick Contino's closing night send-off. I had a glass of wine, which was rare for me, and found myself having FUN! Although I loved every minute I spent at the club, and had laughs with the acts and the staff, clients, and my partners (and I had some of the coolest partners in the world), I hadn't felt like this in I don't know how long. And then up walked Kay. "Anybody sitting here?" she asked. I was at the bar with Dick Contino and his lady but there was an open seat next to me. Kay was NICE. I liked that. She wasn't very smart, but I hadn't been around nice in years, so she started hanging around. She was a server at the club, and my partner Lenny Green, when he heard about it, gave me an earful! In his world, you don't date "the help"! That's exactly what the old prick said. To think I idolized this man. This was now three weeks or so since the violent breakup. I didn't know it, but the evil ex was talking to Lenny, telling him stories, and he must've been buying them. So, Lenny, to drive home his point that my judgment has slipped, told me that he heard that I was drinking and doing cocaine. And he leaned in close and asked, "Are you"? I wasn't, but the clouds were rolling in. But I was too happy then to notice. It was as if a curtain had been lifted and a new world opened up. Suddenly, the staff at the club was friendly. The guys in the house band would come to my apartment after the show and hang out until the wee hours. And this really nice lady was hanging around—no drama, no games. I was enjoying myself socially for the first time in years!

I can't remember a time when I was more content.

The club was doing great. We were averaging 80 percent every week night and sold out on the weekend shows. We were the talk of the town! We not only drew local attention by presenting great name talent, but when the iconic Chicago Cubs broadcaster Harry Caray collapsed in the club on Valentine's Day as he was being sung to and honored, dying in my arms before being resuscitated only to die two days later in the hospital, well, that put Basin Street West on the national news for days! I was working twelve-plus hours a day and loving every minute. We were fast approaching the close of the season, an abbreviated first season, as we started late by opening in January. I had mapped out the next year with Lenny, and we were going full steam ahead. We had opened in a rush, and with short money. All the partners knew that an additional round of investments would be needed at some point shortly after opening, and that time as it turned out, was going to be during our hiatus. I was able to stretch the initial capitalization that far, and literally out of cash flow from day one.

You see, all of the initial money was spent on the remodel and legal, accounting, advertising, and artists' deposits. When we opened the doors on January 6, 1998, we had about $198 in the Basin Street West bank account. Now that was something! Anyway, one of the civilian partners, a real pushy loudmouth Greek named George, had been trying to get me to hire his son as a restaurant manager. This young man was a great-looking kid. He could have been a model, but beyond that, he was useless. He had no experience, no desire to work, nothing. Just a rich, pushy, bastard for a father who figured he could buy his kid a job. Well, not with me.

And without realizing it, a second powerful enemy was beginning to line up against me; the first being Peter Marshall, and now Lenny, who was listening to lies from a very malicious ex-girlfriend was unbeknownst to me, starting to mistrust me.

I issued the financial statements to the shareholders in preparation for an upcoming board meeting. George, unbeknownst to me, went to the restaurant and removed checkbooks, copied only checks that showed me writing checks for cash, cash that would be used to pay out server tips that were on credit card slips that were reimbursed when the credit card deposits were made. Then he called a secret meeting of the shareholders, excluding me, the largest shareholder, in order to present his "proof" that I was stealing money from the club. You see, he never showed that the money was deposited on the credit card slips. He just put fear in their little hearts. The fact that all of this was strictly against our partnership agreement didn't seem to matter. My celebrity partners immediately turned against me, fearing a scandal, and happily put George the Greek in control. Sadly, he and his son, who immediately started as a manager, had no idea what to do, and what could have been a huge success died a mere two weeks later. But not for me. Not when, after having been front-page news as a good guy now accused of going bad... no, it was rough on me. So now three years into this deal, my deal, I'm locked out of my own club and publicly accused of theft!

To make matters worse, that nice young woman Kay, after two months of dating, told me that she was pregnant. And just like that, I wasn't so content, but once again, I do the "right thing." She moved in, and I didn't leave the apartment for four months! I didn't realize it until one day, very gently, she told me that. I was shocked! Four months! I did go out to see my attorney, but that was it.

I had turned down all social invitations; apparently there had been many. I was in a fog of depression. I was living with this woman, nice as she was, whom I hardly knew. I was out of work, publicly shamed, and broke. I had put all my eggs into the Basin Street West "basket," and that basket had been unfairly and unlawfully taken from me. I had an open and shut case, according to my attorney. You see, the very thick agreement that was drawn up specifically said that there could not be any meeting that would exclude a board member, especially one who was being accused of a wrongdoing, whereby he or she could defend themselves. My partners had clearly violated that part of the agreement. They also, through their new leader, George the Greek, told the entire staff that I was let go because I had stolen money from the club! This leaked to the press and was all over town in a New York minute! Yeah, it looked like I had an ironclad case!

The lawsuit against the partners was the only thing that gave me hope. Kay was waiting tables and getting bigger by the day, and I as far as my getting a job, no one in town would touch me! My attorney loved it, saying that it added damages to our case, but he wasn't the one eating beans! For over a year, I looked for work, hustled what I could while I became a reluctant father for the second time.

I welcomed our daughter, who was, and remains a bright spot in my wonderful life. So, throughout this year and half, my attorney built a solid case, a case that he feels is worth a ton. After all, he said, I lost the club (which was thriving), I lost the prospect of the Marcus Hotel deal, and most importantly, I lost my reputation. I was also suing people who were very wealthy—and powerful. It was the powerful part that ultimately got me... or more to the point, I suspect, my rotten attorney! As we approached a pivotal point, my independent attorney in his one-man office with me as his big client FORGOT to file my papers with the court.

And my case was thrown out.

At the same time, he personally filed for bankruptcy and was deemed insolvent. He turned in his license to practice law, leaving me totally high and dry! I can't prove it, but it sure smells like somebody got paid off! This was a multi-million-dollar suit! I'm sure that rat bastard attorney would have (may have?) taken a fraction of that to miss the filing date! For years, just for giggles, every so often, I would call this asshole (who still lives in Palm Springs) just to make him nervous, and it always did. Hey, I got a laugh out of it—it's all I had!

Saying hello to actor Dick Van Patten, who came to see a show at BSW.

BASIN STREET WEST

With Basin Street West partners, Lenny Green and Peter Marshall

Left: Clowning around with comedian
Charlie Callas after his show

BASIN STREET
WEST

Below: With Ernest Borgnine
and Frank Gorshin.

175

Right:
Hanging out after Frank's opening night

BASIN STREET WEST

Below:
With Mort Sahl,
the Father of Political Satire

Left:
Academy Award Winner Richard
Dreyfuss dropped by to catch a show

BASIN
STREET
WEST

Below:
At Basin Street with Lenny Green and
The Mills Brothers.

BASIN STREET WEST

Below:
With The Modernaires, following their performance

Chapter 13

THE COMEBACK

In spite of my being depressed and labeled a thief, once I had pulled myself together enough, a man I had met while at Basin Street West gave me a call. He had some ideas and thought I would fit into them. His name was Bobby Roberts.

I met Bobby Roberts when Mort Sahl, the father of political satire, played Basin Street West. Bobby was Mort's manager. As I recall, we got along alright. During Mort's weeklong performance, Mort and I spent a lot of time together. Mort was ducking Lenny Green's constant invitations to lunch, dinner, drinks, anything and everything. You see, many years before, back in the 1960s, Lenny had booked Mort into the original Basin Street East, and Lenny was trying to recreate the old days, but Mort had little patience for it. He wasn't interested in chit-chat with Lenny's country club set, so Mort quietly sidled up to me. Without Lenny knowing it, I would meet Mort for breakfast and lunch, take him shopping, have him to my apartment for dinner.... We hung out most of the week that he was in town, and we became pretty friendly. Bobby, who lived and worked in Beverly Hills, came down twice that week to make sure that his client, but more importantly, his friend of more than forty years, Mort, was being properly cared for. It was my relationship with Mort, and perhaps a good word or two from him, that prompted Bobby to call me. Bobby Roberts personified show business! He started out as a dancer, and as a young man, was part of the famous dance team "The Dunhills." Later, along with Lou Adler, he formed Dunhill Records, which became a major recording company with such stars on its roster as The Mamas and the Papas, Three Dog Night, and Jimmy Buffett, among others. Then they sold the label to ABC, and it became ABC/Dunhill Records. Bobby also produced the cult movie classics Death Wish and Death Wish II starring Charles Bronson. Also, he was the personal manager to Ann-Margaret, Richard Pryor, and others. His list of clients and accomplishments goes on and on, yet, he called me! Seems he had an idea...

Bobby and Mort believed that the Palm Springs area was the perfect spot for acts like Mort, and I had proved it at Basin Street West. Mort, having worked at the club, felt that whatever caused it to close wasn't my doing, and that I had both show business and local knowledge. They wanted to work with me and develop a show around Mort, initially. Later, we'd grow, add other acts maybe, who knows, become another Basin Street! At this point, about a year had passed since the club had closed, the press had all but stopped running stories about the club, and the civilians had, for the most part, forgotten. I still felt the glare of their stares on the back of my neck (or maybe I just imagined this), but Bobby and Mort felt that enough time had passed, and it was time to get to work again. I was more than ready! For a year or more, I'd been shunned by my former friends and associates, embarrassed to be seen. Now, suddenly I felt redeemed! A Hollywood icon and a comedic genius wanted to work with me! ME! I was BACK! Not all the way, but I knew right then, right when I got that first call from Bobby Roberts, that somehow, things were turning around.

I scoured the town for a suitable venue to showcase Mort, and time after time, came up empty. I was getting pretty down, thinking that my comeback wasn't going so well when I had a crazy idea. I recalled that Sorrentino's, that classic Italian mainstay of the desert whose upholstery I had redone all those years ago, had a garden area that just might work as a performance venue. Mary Sorrentino had all but retired and had handed the business to her half-brained son Billy. Billy, in all his wisdom, had taken a business that his parents had built into a piece of Palm Springs history and was running on autopilot, and had run it into the ground. This was a man of forty who had a high-pitched, loud, whiny voice that would give a woodpecker a headache! When I suggested that we convert the side patio into a dining area with a stage for Mort, the Sorrentino's viewed it as the idea that would revive their business and return them to the glory days of old! Because the patio would only seat fifty for dinner and the show, and we were only planning three shows a week, I thought they were being overly excited about the projections, but who was I to rain on their parade? Once I had the okay from the Sorrentino's, I called Bobby and told him my crazy idea: "There's a patio that we can seat fifty for a show and dinner. It's a nice garden setting, and next door is an office building that the Sorrentino's own, and it's empty. From the second-floor office window, I can shine a follow spotlight on Mort. I can make this work!

181

Bobby, who I was afraid might think my idea was too nuts, LOVED IT! It was different, and that was one thing he felt would work in our favor. We'd bill it as "Mort Sahl in the Sorrentino's Gardens!" He applauded my ingenuity and that gave my very bruised self-esteem a much-needed boost. Maybe I WAS back!

The "Gardens" were severely overgrown. I don't think anyone had been out there in years. Billy Sorrentino's job was to get it cleaned up and the patio furniture spruced up so that we could proudly present a top-drawer show. But working with Billy was almost impossible. He'd get halfway through a task and get distracted, move onto something else, make mistakes, make excuses—he was a mess. In order to meet deadlines, the week before we opened, I actually went over there with a couple of guys and some gardening equipment to trim the bougainvillea and mini palms. He hadn't even cleaned up the landscaping, the cheap bastard!

He wasn't just cheap, I think he was broke. His father had passed. His mother, who had been the face, brains, and backbone of the restaurant for decades, was retired, but worse, was very ill. And, truth be told, he was an idiot. I'm not being mean. Some people are just asses. Opinionated, loud-mouthed, obnoxious idiots. You've met the type before—he was one of them. Nobody liked him, some people put up with him, if they had to, but he was an incompetent moron. So, with Bobby in Beverly Hills, the heavy lifting fell on me, and after having been in hibernation, I was happy to be out and to be busy. But I was not happy with the Sorrentinos and a bit concerned that they may not deliver. Mort, Bobby, and I had dinner there a few times; the food was great, same old recipes that made them famous and a favorite of Sinatra's. But now our concern was the service. We knew that we were going to fill each of the fifty seats that would be our capacity. That may not sound like a lot of people, but it is a lot of people to serve drinks and dinner to, all at the same time. Not only was Billy incompetent, he and his staff (who, in all fairness, were very professional), were not used to serving large parties. Bad combination; easy solution. I had Billy hire a few former Basin Street West folks for the shows. They knew what to do. They ran it smoothly.

My knowledge of the media market and the people in it helped a lot Mort Sahl appealed to an older demographic, and that demo was easily reached using just two or three radio stations. As an added bonus, I knew the owners or general managers of the stations and could buy advertising for next to nothing! I also wrote the copy for the ads and recorded the commercials with Mort. So, for some sweat equity as a gardener and a spotlight operator, copywriter, voice talent and promotions man, I was partners with Mort Sahl and Bobby Roberts. Nice. I was very proud. And ready to have a hit show.

And a hit it was!

I hired the Whitey Mitchell Trio to warm up the crowd with some straight-ahead jazz. Whitey was a former comedy writer on shows like Get Smart and was a good bass player, but nothing like his famous brother, Red Mitchell. The trio would play during dinner, then Mort would work his magic. We sold out every Friday, Saturday, and Sunday for three straight months, until Mort got as fed up with Whitey and Billy as I did. I had been friendly with Whitey and his wife Marilyn, but working with him was another story. What a pain in the ass! He acted like the show was about HIM, and Mort didn't like that Toss in Billy, the idiot man, running around messing with things that didn't need messing with. And after a while, it just wasn't worth it. But it had been a hit, and that's what I needed. It had me pumped up and believing in myself again, but the cash flow was gone.

At that time, the general manager of Palm Springs Mercedes Benz called to let me know they had an opening in the sales department. I had stopped in more than a year before when I was persona non grata, figuring I had a chance to get a job because I knew the people there. They just didn't have anything back then. Not that I wanted to sell cars, but with the "Mort" show closing and a wife and baby to feed, I had no choice. It was a good job, and one that would allow me time to keep pushing projects with Bobby Roberts. Bobby and I were solid by now. We had developed a friendship and trust that I had rarely seen. On my days off, I'd often meet him in Beverly Hills to discuss a deal or to meet with an investor, of which he had many. We were always looking for a way to make a quick buck, but more importantly, we were seeking an opportunity in the desert that would last a while. Every time I would get an idea or hear something about someone, I'd call Bobby and we'd hash it out. Since Bobby had seen the merit in the crazy Sorrentino Gardens idea, I wasn't afraid to run anything or anyone by him.

One day, I caught wind that an Indian casino, Spotlight 29, was unhappy with their entertainment director. I happened to know this guy, so I scheduled lunch with him. He was as unhappy with the casino as they apparently were with him. Two months remained on his contract, which left little time for us to move in.

I called Bobby immediately after that lunch and gave him all the info, and the very next day we were sitting with the Chief of the Band of 29 Mission Indians. My resume, which by most standards read pretty well, was paled by that of the famous producer Bobby Roberts, but to have both of us willing to co-direct the entertainment department was a no-brainer for the Chief. He signed us on the spot. We agreed to a one-year contract for $120,000, payable in monthly installments of $10,000: $5,000 to me, and $5,000 to Bobby. Not bad. Of course, because I was the local man on the ground, once again, the daily activities and heavy lifting fell on my shoulders, but I was happy that it did. And although I had the selling gig at the Mercedes store, I knew that, with Bobby's help, I could do both. Since I was knocking down an average of $7,500 per month selling cars, I was reluctant to give that up. I approached management at the Mercedes dealership and presented a marketing plan whereby they could benefit by my association with the casino as a sponsor of our shows. They liked it, as did the casino. Everything was fitting into place. I/we had a production office at the casino, and a really nice theater that seated approximately 2,500 people for each show. With Bobby's help, we were able to plan and book the next year's schedule within thirty days of signing on. The rest was a downhill cruise.

Every show that we put on was a sellout. Not just a full house, but tickets sold to the right people: people with money who would gamble. The "drop," which was the take from the casino on our show nights, was the largest the tribe had ever seen! Debbie Reynolds. Chicago. Ray Charles, Frank Sinatra Jr. with Mort Sahl, Chubby Checker. Neil Sedaka. Bill Cosby. Carrot Top. We made it look easy, so easy that after seven months, the Chief called me into his office and told me that I was to train his stepson to basically take our place. This young man, nice as he was, knew nothing about show business. His meteoric rise in his tribe's business so far had taken him from customer service to the lofty position that he currently held; he was in charge of the coffee carts! The Chief, ever so grateful for the fine work that Bobby and I had done, felt that we could train, in just a few months, this young man to do what we could do. I politely told him that show business, like most businesses, had its own specialties, its own language even, and in a few months, I couldn't train even the smartest man in the world. It's more about contacts and pricing knowledge, I told him, but he insisted. I suggested that his stepson work for a year or two with us, in order to learn these contacts and how to structure shows and promotions and advertising.

But it became clear that the stepson was in and we were out. To prove that his decision was the correct one, the Chief had us book a rap show that consisted of acts picked by this coffee cart genius! I warned the Chief strongly against this show. I clearly laid out that this show would attract the wrong demographic. Fights would break out, driving his regular gamblers out of the casino. I also bet that they wouldn't sell more than 500 tickets.

Being right on all accounts cemented our departure as entertainment directors. In the settlement meeting, the stepson accused me of somehow making all of my predictions come true. If only I was that powerful! But the Chief was that powerful, and rich. Rich enough to weather this and any other financial gaffe his idiot stepchild would make. Following the meeting, the Chief, who was a fine gentleman, took me into his office and thanked me for a job well done. He didn't need to explain. I understood. He called his secretary and ordered a check in the amount due Bobby and me to satisfy the balance of our contract. He was very gracious as he gave me the check and shook my hand.

Only in show business.

As I was cleaning out my office, I gave Bobby a call. He listened quietly as I explained what happened. When I was done, all Bobby said was, "Fuck 'em. Call me later." And he hung up.

My experience in show business had taught me that no deal lasted forever. I was always looking for the next idea, the next show, the next... anything! My drive to Spotlight 29 Casino took me past the new tennis stadium that was just emerging in Indian Wells. This was a world-class tennis facility that was being developed to house professional tournaments and was in every way a dream concert venue to a wild-thinking, no-holds-barred guy like me. One day, on a whim, I pulled into the stadium's parking lot. I got out and walked around. The grounds were enormous. Parking for thousands. I decided to see if I could find who ran the place, because I'd already made up my mind: we were doing major concerts here! The reception area was lush and, even though not quite finished, stunning. The executive area overlooked the stadium. The magnitude and quality was breathtaking. Whoever put this together knew what they were doing. It must have appeared as if I was lost as I took in what looked like heaven to me, when a secretary asked if she could help me. Just then, Ray Moore, my former next-door neighbor from Indian Wells Country Club, walked in. Big hellos! We went through the usual greetings and caught up a bit. Then he invited me into his office —the president's office!

Sometimes, things just go your way. I got to my car and gave Bobby a call. All I said was, "I found our next deal. We're in the concert business."

"What show do you want to do?" he asked.

"Pavarotti.

He was silent for a beat, then asked, "Where are you?" After I laid it out, he became more excited than I'd ever seen. My knowing one of the partners was a giant stroke of luck. Walking into what had turned into a meeting that had all but cemented Bobby and my relationship with the Indian Wells Tennis Garden was serendipity! Bobby couldn't believe our good luck! He was still reeling from the disrespectful way we had been treated by the casino. He felt that this was more on the level that we should be working, anyway. We now had a venue that could seat not 2,500, like the casino, but up to 10,000 people.

Pavarotti. Yeah, Bobby liked the idea. So did everyone.

News of the team of Roberts and Marin as concert producers at the fabulous Indian Wells Tennis Garden presenting the world-renowned tenor, Luciano Pavarotti, set the town a-rockin'! Bobby, one who was highly sensitive to matters of respect, felt that both he and I were being redeemed; he, in that the casino disrespected both of us, and with me, the whole Basin Street West fiasco. I was too busy to care about that at this point. As well as putting on the Pavarotti show, we had two other shows to produce. I had learned long before that to put investors into only one show was just too dangerous, even a show that looked as solid as the Pavarotti show. Plus, when you had such a strong headliner, it only made sense to tie that show to a series of shows. It brought in more investment dollars, more production fees and spread out the risk. Good for everyone involved. Plus, I was still at the Mercedes store, but not for long. As I mentioned, the news of Bobby and I producing a Pavarotti concert was the biggest news in the

Palm Springs area since, well, Basin Street West! I was being interviewed on TV and radio, and for stories in the paper, it was crazy! All of a sudden, there were streams of people coming to see me at the Mercedes store—for everything but a car!

They wanted tickets or interviews or favors of one kind or another. My phone kept ringing and I was being paged constantly. Of course, I had discussed promotional opportunities and marketing plans for the Mercedes dealership, but this time they passed. The traffic I generated at the dealership became a distraction, and no matter what I did to dissuade it, the excitement around the shows had a life of its own and people, sometimes people I barely knew, came by looking for a discounted ticket or some other favor. It was a circus. It couldn't go on. Long before the first of our three concerts of the season, I was, not so politely, told to leave the sacred grounds of Palm Springs Mercedes Benz.

At first, it was almost a blessing, as it freed up precious time. I was doing fine money-wise. The production budgets that I was charged with designing provided for all of our expenses plus we had back-end participation, meaning that Bobby and I would share in the profits. Now I had more time to manage all the aspects of this concert series, as well as lay the groundwork for the next year's productions.

Bobby took care of everything involving the investors. He had a Rolodex full of the richest and most powerful people on the planet. It took less than a week to secure the financing for our first three concerts at the Tennis Garden. The initial concert series lineup was Los Lobos with El Chicano, then a Christian show featuring Third Day and The Newsboys, two chart- topping Christian groups at the time. Both of these shows were presented to a smaller audience, as we only used the lower portion of the stadium, which sat approximately 4,500 people. For the Pavarotti show, we opened up the top level of the stadium, increasing the capacity to nearly 10,000. With such strong shows and the support of this incredible venue, Bobby and I felt like we had found a home. Ray Moore and his partner, Charlie Pasarell, welcomed us completely. We were given a beautiful production office and were regarded as partners. As far as any entertainment issues were concerned, we were the guys. We were in this for the long haul.

The Los Lobos/El Chicano show sold out. Perfect. Everything went as planned. Next up was Pavarotti. Again, sold out. The show was phenomenal! The front-row seats, although pricey, $500 each, came with the bonus of attending the after party. The guest list at this event had everyone from Lee Iacocca and Barbara Sinatra to Robert Wagner. Stars and captains of industry, politicians and the desert's well-to-do all "made the scene" that night. We had to hold the opening of the show for forty-five minutes because of the unprecedented traffic jam that was caused! Never before had so many cars tried to get to the same location at the same time! This was the worst traffic jam in the history of Indian Wells, California! In spite of all the planning meetings with the city and the police to address this very concern, traffic was at a standstill! We had no choice but to hold up the show. We announced to those already there that there would be a delay and radioed the message to the police on the street so that they would take their time.

In the end, it all worked out beautifully, and Pavarotti put on a show the likes of which I'd never seen, and I'm no rookie! The after party was great. The band consisted of members of the Johnny Carson's Tonight Show band; my dear old friends, Conte Condoli and Frankie Capp, had the crowd swinging! What a night! Even my old partner from Basin Street West, Jack Jones was there and had the class to come up to me and apologize for not supporting me when I was wrongly accused, and to congratulate me on such a great concert! Jack was a couple of years late; his speaking up at the time may have saved me from that world of hurt, but I appreciated the apology, nonetheless.

The final show of our inaugural season was the Christian concert. This show I was against from the start, but one of our investors, who lived in the desert, wanted it. He was a member of a huge church that happened to sit on the same property as the Tennis Stadium. That church had 10,000 followers worship there every weekend—10,000! This gentleman arranged meetings with the pastor, who was so excited by this that he agreed to promote this show to his congregation. He would do this and that, and let us do that and this, and praise the lord and all will be wonderful!

Well, he didn't do anything.

At about this time, the news broke of the Christian pastor and a woman, who was not his wife, taking long leisurely hot tubs in the nude, complete with pictures. Praise the lord—and pray for ticket sales! That's what we were doing. With this scandal going on, not too many folks from that mega church wanted anything to do with him or anything he promoted. So, to appease an investor, and against my better judgment (it's not that I'm against religion, but I've just never had any luck with religious-based shows), we had a loser on our hands! Do you have any idea what a joy it is to listen to musicians preach from the stage, testifying for hours about how they have been saved, while I'm trying to figure out how much we're going to lose on this show? We dropped $35,000! It was the worst! Almost as bad as my rap show experience at the casino.

Overall, the series of concerts made Bobby and me and our investors quite a nice profit. Nice enough that we had the investment money for the next season in the bank, and Bobby's and my future as concert promoters looked as bright as any star in the sky. Our 2001–2002 concert season at the beautiful Indian Wells Tennis Garden was going to be bigger and even more exciting than our first season. We had deposits in for Andrea Bocelli; Alan Jackson; and Crosby, Stills and Nash. Of course, we were still in discussions with other acts for later in the season, but these were the main shows, with Bocelli being the anchor show. All summer we spent laying the groundwork for the coming season, finalizing agreements with our investors and the venue, designing sponsorship packages and of course, artist contracts. By the end of August, we had it dialed in. We decided not to formally announce the season's lineup until mid-September, at which time we would begin a modest advertising campaign that would increase as the desert filled back up with seasonal residents.

The morning of September 11 was busy. Although it was mentioned to me on each phone call I had that morning, I didn't grasp the severity of what was being said to me about "planes flying into the Trade Center in New York!" I was so busy preparing for a lunch meeting with Andrea Bocelli's conductor that I just didn't get it... I was thinking that maybe a Cessna or two crashed. But when I finally got to our meeting, which was at a country club restaurant, and sat down and looked at the television to see what had happened, I said to the kind gentleman who had driven from Los Angeles to meet me that our business was most likely finished. Sadly, I was correct. When there is an act of terror, contracts get cancelled. And that's exactly what happened. Our season was gone. People lost their lives that day, or their loved ones. We as a nation lost so much. Please understand that I am not diminishing that at all when I personalize this. I/we only lost money and related things, but they are real, too. Important, also. For Bobby and me, that day ended our season, but not our responsibility. We had deposits with major agencies for these acts that now had cancelled; money we had to get back to our investors.

We no longer had income, just responsibilities.

In this photo, I'm with Luciano Pavarotti and co-producer Bobby Roberts after Pavarotti's incredible concert April 6, 2001, at the Indian Wells Tennis Gardens. The concert was sponsored by The City of Indian Wells and The Desert Sun, and was one of the most gratifying events of my career.

INDIAN WELLS TENNIS GARDENS

Bobby Roberts, Francesco Quinn, Me and Greg from Indian Wells Tennis Garden

INDIAN WELLS TENNIS GARDENS

Left:
Here I am with Rock & Roll Hall of Fame inductee Chubby Checker, after the show.

SPOTLIGHT 29
CASINO

Below:
Here, I'm with business partner and dear friend Bobby Roberts and Debbie Reynolds, following her sold out show that we produced at Spotlight 29 Casino in 1999. This was a great reunion for all of us, as both Bobby and I hadn't seen Debbie in years.

Above:
Fooling around after a show with
one of the nicest "tough guys" I've
ever met, actor Wes Studi.

SPOTLIGHT
29
CASINO

Left:
Never a dull moment with
Carrot-Top! Another fun show.

SPOTLIGHT 29
CASINO

Visiting with both Keely Smith and
Neil Sedaka after Neil's show at
Spotlight 29 Casino.

SPOTLIGHT 29 CASINO

Below:
Bobby Roberts, agent Steve Garey, Frank Sinatra Jr., Me, and Mort Sahl
following a wonderful concert.

Above:
Bobby and Me with the bands El Chicano and Malo

SPOTLIGHT 29 CASINO

Below:
I'm with the band Chicago

Chapter 14

SOULLESS

That "nice" woman whom I did the "right thing" with and married had become not as nice, because she'd turned out to be a full-blown alcoholic. We hardly spoke and had been in separate rooms nearly from the start. My little girl was the only reason I even stayed in the house. Bobby, who had a slight cough since the day we met, now had a cough that had gotten pretty bad, and he'd gone from having boundless energy to spending days on end in bed. I knew something was wrong, but he wasn't talking. I managed to stay away from my old friend cocaine all through the Basin Street West days and after, but once the mother of my daughter fell into the cups, that old familiar underlying feeling of discontent found its way back to the surface, and I started using again. Mostly meth, this time. So suddenly, I have no work, a sick partner, an alcoholic wife, and I was lost again. I didn't know what to do! It seemed that every time I knocked on the door of success, it opened and closed so fast it caused suction, and I got sucked out!

The next year and a half or so was spent cleaning up old commitments and trying to get new deals started. Bobby's health was deteriorating, although he wouldn't cop to it. Old school. Never let on that you're sick. My health, mostly my attitude, was at an all-time low. I couldn't kick the feeling that I was sinking. I'd been down before, but never had I felt this hopeless. Sure, I put on a good face, but inside, I was cracking. The deals that Bobby and I were working on, for the most part, were ones that took time to develop. Sure, we had little things go down, bringing in a few thousand here and there, but the larger deals didn't fall like they did before. The money I had stacked up was dwindling. My hobby of "turning" classic cars brought in a few bucks here and there, but all in all, nowhere near what I had become accustomed to. I was full of regret for the first time in my life. I regretted buying our house in this mid-level country club; I regretted marrying a woman I hardly knew; and, although I loved my little daughter, I regretted terribly having to share her with this drunken woman. And I regretted, once again, that I was using.

I was lost. Living a lie. Pretending that everything was okay. That's what I was taught. Keep it in, don't let on, because if people know that you're sick or broke or just down on your luck or depressed (or using again), they won't touch you! It's like they think it's contagious! So, with a happy face and a positive tone, I continued every day to search for opportunities for me and Bobby. With each deal's delay or failure, I became more desperate. When Bobby would cancel or reschedule a meeting, I felt more anxious. Nothing in my life seemed to flow.

Everything seemed to be at odds with my hopes and plans. As I said before, I felt lost. I remember talking to the one trusted friend I could share anything with, Rocco Presutti. It felt good to be able to tell someone everything that was on my mind, to unload the burden that I was carrying hidden beneath my practiced smile; hidden deeply under my dark habits. After revealing all that tortured me, I was somewhat relieved, as if I'd gone to confession.

Rocco, after taking a minute to absorb what I'd laid on him, responded with the wisdom only Rocco, God love him, could provide. In response to my business concerns, he simply told me to keep at it, reassuring me by saying: "I've never known anyone that always lands on their feet like you do." Well, that made me feel good, you know, a bit. It was nice to know that after all I'd been through—and believe me, Rocco had seen or at least knew about my ups and downs—that he believed in me.

But when it came to my home life (me in one room, her drunk in another), his response was, "Does she cook and keep the house nice?"

Yes, I answered.

"Does she look after your daughter?"

"Yes, until about 8:00 pm when she passes out," I answered.

"What are you bitching about? Sounds like you've got the perfect situation: a live-in nanny that cooks and cleans that you can fuck whenever you want to!"

With this, we both broke into hysterical laughter, something not uncommon whenever we talk, but something that I really needed at that moment.

Bobby and I had focused much of our time on acquiring a small movie studio in a town called Santa Clarita, about 30 miles northwest of Hollywood. Every aspect of the Santa Clarita Studios deal made sense, making it relatively easy for us to arrange the financing. The purchase price, although somewhat inflated, was within reach. The financials that were presented to us showed an underused facility, one that was barely hanging on. That was something we were sure that we could change. After six or seven months of negotiations, when we were very close to closing, another prospective buyer surfaced, which pissed off Bobby. I'd never seen him like this. We were in a meeting, expecting to settle the issues so that we could close the sale, when we were told of this "other offer." Bobby immediately stood up, grabbing my sleeve and pulling me up, and said to this man, in his customary soft voice, "You've just wasted months of our time. You are being dishonest, and we won't deal this way. Let's go, Peter." And we started for the door. When the owner of the studio tried to stop us, Bobby simply said, "Honor our deal, or go fuck yourself." Softly spoken. No yelling. No arms flailing. Just that. "Honor our deal or go fuck yourself." We leaned on my car in the parking lot of the Santa Clarita Studios as we tried to console ourselves. This would have been such a wonderful opportunity for both of us, but it wasn't looking good. I had great respect for Bobby. He knew when to cut his losses. He took no shit from anybody, and I liked that. Me, I was feeling so desperate and insecure that I probably would have taken a softer line, and had the same result, only I wouldn't have had my self-respect intact.

Lesson learned. Thank you, Bobby Roberts.

So instead of house hunting in Santa Clarita that afternoon as originally planned, I drove back to the desert with a darkness inside that I just couldn't shake, and wouldn't shake really, for a very long time.

That feeling of discontent and uncertainty that had been growing so slowly over the years, bubbling deep in my soul, was now working its way to the surface. The drive from Santa Clarita to Palm Springs seemed to take forever. I couldn't stop thinking about the lost opportunity we just saw pulled off the table—an opportunity that would have taken me out of the desert and into the heart of the movie and video and music video production business. But no. That loop of thought of what could have been wouldn't stop, and when finally, it did, it was replaced with the horrifying repeating theme of me, trapped in my present circumstances, forever a bridesmaid at the door of success. I physically felt as if I was sinking. I can't describe it any other way. I hid the truth about my personal life from everyone (except Rocco), which takes a toll in its own way, and my professional prospects in show business were nowhere to be seen. I was running out of money, and Bobby, although he was trying to put on a strong front, was just running out of energy. I had an overpowering urge to run away. I had to get out! If I move, get a fresh start, I could stop using these damn drugs and get back on track! Over the next few weeks I became desperate to get out of the desert. Bobby and I looked into situations for me in Los Angeles with people and companies that he knew, but nothing was solid enough to move on. Finally, when I was down to my last $1,200, I called an old friend, Al Perlin, that I had worked with at that BMW dealership in San Diego all those years ago who now ran a Lexus store there.

We had stayed in touch over the years. Al had enjoyed hearing of my escapades and especially of my success and was saddened when he heard about my current situation. However, Lady Luck wasn't done with me yet. It just so happened that he had an opening in the sales department, and if I could be there the next day, and pass a drug test, I had the job. Shit! A drug test! I asked if the test was written to oral. He laughed and told me to meet him at 9:30 in the morning, and he'd have a job for me worth $90k or better. Man was I ever in a jam! I had to get this job, although in my heart of hearts, I felt that selling cars was admitting I'd given up on all of my dreams. I needed the money and a change of scene, but there was no way I could pass a drug test. As fate would have it, as I was trying to solve this dilemma, a man named Ed Miller stopped by. Ed would help me from time to time with my classic cars. Ed looked like a biker or a bouncer. He was maybe six feet tall and stocky, barrel chested and covered in tattoos of women in S&M positions doing things to each other... you get the picture. Add a well-groomed Mohawk to the mix, and you have one scary looking mofo! He looked like a mean Jeanie who had escaped from that magical bottle. But under this unruly exterior was a very kind, gentle, drug-free unemployed man who had been complaining about his life in the desert.

"Hey, Ed. What are you doin' tomorrow?"

We left for San Diego bright and early the next morning in his big Lincoln Continental. We had devised a plan to beat the drug test, even doing a practice run the night before. But the plan wasn't foolproof, and I was nervous. Not only did I need this job, but I couldn't stand the embarrassment of my old friend knowing that I was using if I failed the test. After meeting my pal, the big Lexus boss, we went to the testing facility. It was on the second floor. On the first floor was a restroom, where Ed filled a condom with the needed "clean" sample, which he quickly handed to me. I put it in my tidy whities (I wore 'em just for this special occasion) and I hurried to the elevator, knowing that I had to get the "sample" into the lab's testing cup while was it still hot enough. As the elevator door opened, some guy cut me off, blasting his way in, and when we arrived to the floor where the lab is, he rudely pushed passed me and was first in the lab, and first to get tested. Then as I was waiting, I noticed that the condom that was stuffed in my drawers was starting to leak, leaving a small but ever so slowly growing wet spot on my crotch.

Oh, man, was I ever getting nervous.

Finally, the attendant came to get me, and thank God that she obviously hated her job, because she hardly looked at me. She put me in a bathroom, told me what to do, and left. I took a toothpick from my shirt pocket, pulled the leaking condom from my underwear (yuk!), poked a hole in it, filled the cup with big Ed's clean urine, and gave the lab a sample that I prayed was still warm enough. The totally disinterested lab attendant, after ten or fifteen harrowing minutes, came out to tell me that I passed. Then, she said, with a wry smile, that I should see a doctor—because based on my body temperature, I'm barely alive. And then she winked. She actually winked at me! I grabbed the sheet that gave me a drug-free vote of confidence and headed for the bathroom downstairs where I scrubbed and scrubbed my hands, but I still felt like I had traces of "Ed" on me! After taking my buddy out to a celebratory breakfast, we went to the Lexus dealership, where I presented the paperwork. I also asked if there might be a job for Ed. There was. We both started work two days later.

One funny thing. When we got back to my house in the desert, we were greeted at the door by my sweet dog, Moxie. She sniffed Ed first, then immediately turned her head and sniffed my crotch, then quickly back to him then to me and back again and finally she stepped back and just shook her head in confusion, giving Ed and me a belly laugh to end a long but successful day.

Ed and I checked in for work early that Friday morning, me for my sales duties, and Ed for his porter duties. We drove from the desert together in his car, so that I could leave my car at home for my daughter's mother, should she need it. I had sold my regular car long before and had been driving whatever classic car I was restoring. So, Ed was the wheelman and I covered the motel rooms while we figured out our next move. Compared to Ed, I was rich. He had no cash. I still had about $800, but that wouldn't cover the bills that would be due again in a couple of weeks … and with motels and gas and two people back home with needs, I was in trouble. I had only one way out. I put my head down and swallowed my pride. I worked my ass off that long weekend and was the top salesperson for the event. The bosses had all kinds of games to play when you sold a car: you'd roll dice or pick a card or throw darts at balloons with pieces of paper in them featuring dollar amounts. Because I was the top salesperson, I played the most games, and won over $2,600 in cash bonuses. Cash! Plus, my commissions, just for the weekend were nearly $3,000!

I hated selling cars, but I gotta tell ya, this kinda money in three days got my attention. I needed a boost. My self-esteem and my bank account were at all-time lows, so my swooping into town, the new guy on the scene, and kicking ass felt good. It felt really good. The big boss man, my old friend who had taken a chance and hired me, was so happy. When I told him that I didn't have a car, he sold me one that had been traded in, a pretty nice Hyundai, for $1,500 cash.

I was starting to feel like a person again. I had wheels, a few bucks in my pocket, next month's bills covered, and two more weeks to make more. Now, to find a place to live. On a lark, I called my old landlord, the man who had rented the house to me in Ocean Beach so many years before. That property had a studio which was a converted one-car garage plus the two-bedroom house in front; it would be perfect. I doubted that it would be available but thought maybe he had other properties. Once again, fate smiled on me. Not only was the house in front available, but so was the studio. "Hey, Ed, you need a place to stay? Have I got a deal for you!" So, I rented the house for my daughter and, as Rocco referred to her, "the nanny," and sublet the studio to Ed. Serendipity. I put our house in the desert up for sale, it sold rather quickly, and we all settled in a mere a block from the beautiful Sunset Cliffs in Ocean Beach, California. With a new leaf to turn over, we all hoped.

My hopes were to make this car business thing as short lived as possible and get back to what I knew and loved, show business. But, as I said earlier, projects that were on the table with Bobby all seemed to be withering. Nothing was jelling, everything was out of sync. I was desperate to land a deal, to get out of this soul-sucking car business, as lucrative as it was. Yet I felt completely tied to Bobby, as if I couldn't do anything on my own. In spite of my self-loathing for being a "car salesman," I worked hard and was a top earner, regularly finishing in the top three every month. I earned accolades, awards, and bonuses.

Yet, nearly every day during my first year at Lexus, Bobby and I would talk by phone, as we always had, planning our next deal or conquest. At least once a month, on my day off I would drive to Beverly Hills and meet him for lunch. It was odd how not so long ago it seemed that we had so much happening, and now nothing was coming our way. Even Bobby's favorite lunch spot, the famous Café Roma, seemed to lose its charm. And although I never said anything, I couldn't help noticing that Bobby was losing weight. His once-strong dancer's body was somehow looking hollow. Not a lot. But I noticed. And when I asked about his increased coughing, he just brushed it off. Never admit that something's wrong. Must be some kind of show biz motto. As close as we were—and we were very close—that's one area that Bobby would never come clean on. His health.

My first year selling at Lexus passed so quickly that it even surprised me. I was very busy. The six-hour shifts often turned to eight or ten hours, and my off hours were still spent building and designing programs and production ideas that Bobby and I might find investors for and taking care of my little girl. Every two weeks I would drive back to the desert and pick up my supply of meth to get me through. I was so strung out, but I had rules that I adhered to regarding my drug use. No needles. Always eat and sleep. These rules kept me alive. I was such a mess, but because of my "rules," I was still able to fool almost everyone. No one really knew that I had a drug problem, or an alcoholic "nanny" at home, or, for that matter, that I had a problem in the world. But I did. And the feeling of failure that haunted me daily as I stood on a car lot waiting to beat the other guys to the next customer; and that kicked in the gut-sick feeling I had when driving home, knowing that I'd be greeted by the "nanny" who, by this time would be slurring her words so badly I could hardly understand her. Then I felt the guilt that overwhelmed me when my beautiful daughter looked up at me with complete love and trust—guilt that I had let her down with my failures.

This terrible fall from grace had taken its toll. I was so far removed from all that had been my reality. From my roots in Los Angeles and Palm Springs. From my friends who, for the most part, I rarely saw. From show business. It had now been three years since I'd produced a concert, and God knows how long since I'd sung! I was like a fish out of water, driven only by the need for income to support my dysfunctional family and fueled by the false energy derived from speed. My dependence on Bobby to break out of my slump and get me back into show business hadn't lessened, although our opportunities were fewer. We continued to speak by phone nearly every day, but my trips to see him became less frequent. When I did see him, his usual tap dancer's light and quick step had slowed noticeably, and the cough had thickened.

But he was fine. Just ask him. Then one weekend, one very busy weekend, I kept meaning to call him. Each time I'd start to, something would interrupt me. That Sunday night, I had a vivid dream, the kind of dream that seems so real that even now I'm not sure that it wasn't. I sat up, awakened by my dear friend Bobby, who was standing at the foot of my bed. He smiled the warmest, sweetest smile and said, "Just wanted you to know that I'm alright, Peter, my boy. I'm alright." He beamed that wonderful smile of his and was gone. All the next day, as busy as I was, I meant to call, but the time got away from me.

That night, I had exactly the same dream, just as vivid, so real. Now, with a feeling of foreboding, first thing in the morning, I finally gave Bobby a call. Lynn, Bobby's wife and one true love, answered his cell phone. Never, in the five-plus years of my calling this phone had anyone other than Bobby answered it. Before Lynn had said a word, my heart began to sink.

"Oh, Peter, I'm so sorry. I have been meaning to call you. Bobby loved you so much. So much more than just a friend and business partner. More like a son..."

"What happened?" I interrupted.

"Bobby died Sunday afternoon," Lynn told me. "He started coughing up blood. We rushed him to the hospital, but there was nothing they could do. He was gone three hours later. I'm so sorry, I've been meaning to call you." After some time, when we both could breathe again, I shared with her my dreams of the previous two nights. She wasn't surprised at all; I was the second person who told her about having had the exact same experience.

Bobby's death was harder for me than any that had come before, even my own father's death hadn't affected me so deeply. We had a relationship unlike anything that I'd known, and with the exclusion of my drug use, one that was open and honest. Bobby believed in me at a time when I was untouchable, and together we accomplished wonderful things. He always took the time to hear my ideas, of which I had many, not all which were good, mind you, and gave me the feeling that I mattered, that, when we spoke, I was the only person in the room. His attention was focused in a way that made me feel important, an equal—equal to a man that had done it all in show business. This generosity of spirit I'd never seen and haven't seen again. He was one of a kind. I loved him very much and miss him every day. But mostly, I'm grateful that Bobby Roberts drove to the desert with Mort Sahl that day back in 1998 to check out our club, Basin Street West. With all the pain that club ended up bringing me, it also brought me one of the greatest friendships and business partnerships of my life.

I was alone. With Bobby gone, I felt completely disconnected from what had been my life: show business. Our planning and plotting during the last couple of years had kept me in the game; at least it allowed me to feel that way. A project we were working on or an idea we were developing could happen with a phone call, but not anymore, not now, not without Bobby. He was the key to everything. I had given away all of my power, although I didn't realize it at the time. I had succumbed to this civilian life that I truly dreaded. It's not that I looked down on it, please don't misunderstand, it's just that I can't thrive there. For me to flow with creative ideas—ideas that launched great performances and clubs and shows and concerts throughout the years—I can't be answering to someone else's dream or demands. I shut down. Close up, withdraw inside. Add to this my unhealthy marriage and my self-hatred for using, and I was at an all-time low Again. Yet, true to the code, I put on a happy face, and did what I could to make as much money as I could, hoping that that would at least give me some feeling of success. It didn't. I was a top seller at work, well liked, the life of the party with show biz stories to impress the customers and with pictures to prove that I wasn't just another bullshit car salesman!

With each passing month I felt as if whatever was creative in me was dying; drying up inside of me. It was a tangible feeling. One that was so strong, that I made an appointment with my doctor. Changes needed to be made. Now. I had been her patient for nearly three years, and, because of my drug use "rules," I had fooled her, too. When I told her that I needed help to quit using speed, she was shocked! I had never given her a reason to test me for drug use. I was twenty pounds overweight, not emaciated. I was well groomed, nicely dressed, gainfully employed, and as charming as a guy with a thirty-year performance background in show business could be. In other words, not your typical druggie. Her normally professional face morphed into one of kindness and understanding. As I broke down, mostly from the relief of unburdening myself of this "secret," she warmly put her arm around me while I sobbed. Then, she offered a potential solution. A new drug, an antidepressant, had great success for this very thing. And for me, thank God, it worked. I never, from that day, took speed again.

And I began to see myself for who I was.

Although that wasn't always such a pretty picture, over the next two years I came to grips with my past. It was my past. A past that had led me to wonderful places with exciting and talented people. A past in which I accomplished magnificent things. My present, by comparison, was a drag. As I said before, I viewed my selling cars as flag of surrender, as if I was a prisoner of my own failure. My home life was another sad situation: my daughter in one bedroom, me in another, and the "nanny" on the couch. It had been like that for years. Semi-peaceful co-existence. But with my sobriety, my wife's drinking became intolerable to me. In an effort to salvage our farce of a marriage, at the suggestion of a friend and coworker, I secretly attended Al-Anon meetings. Any hope of finding answers that would help to heal our badly broken relationship didn't exist there, and I clearly saw that it was time for her to choose; get help, or I'm out.

She tried. She checked in for an in-patient stay or two, but she'd jump right back into a bottle. She had it bad. Finally, after months of telling her that I was going to leave, I did. I rented a room from a woman who had a beautiful townhouse that she hardly lived in. Her fiancé lived in Newport Beach (about 100 miles away), and she'd spend only a day or two each week at home. Having me watch the place was a relief to her, and a relief for me, as well.

A week or so after I moved, my daughter called me. She was crying and needed me to come right away. She said that Mommy wouldn't wake up and she was so scared. "Please, Daddy, come now!" I was at work when she called. It was late afternoon. Her mother had always managed to control her drinking so that she cared for our daughter. She'd get her up and dressed, fed, and off to school in the morning. She'd pick her up after school and get dinner on the table. She kept a clean house and managed usually until after putting her to bed. Then, she'd slip away. Her words would begin to slur and soon, she'd slip into a near-coma until morning. My moving out had put her into a tailspin, which I should have predicted when I calculated my leaving. I had tried to be thorough in my planning, estimating my new expenses and projecting hers. I was sick to death of dealing with her shit and could not wait to get out. But I had to have the money side covered. It looked like it was, barely. My production at work had been slipping over the last few months. I took into account everything except her not being able to care for our daughter.

When I arrived at the house, my daughter met me at the door. The living room was dark as we entered, the drapes pulled. Once my eyes adjusted, I saw my wife, half falling off the couch, half on the floor, passed out. I tried to wake her, but she wouldn't come to. Although this wasn't the first time I'd seen this, it was a first for my daughter—a very upsetting first. I assured her that her mother would be fine, but for now, we'd pack her things and she was coming with me. I packed her up and moved her in with me. The next day, she was enrolled in third grade in a new school and we started a new chapter together.

Chapter 15

MINDLESS AND LOST

I was balancing being a single father to a sweet young girl who had an alcoholic, and now, due to really bad choices on her part, a homeless mother, with maintaining a highly competitive job as my performance declined. This, as you may well imagine, brought about challenges that I was not well prepared for. My bosses were expressing concern about my drop in sales, my "wife" was calling, needing help that I couldn't give her, my daughter didn't understand what was going on with her mother, and why she didn't have a house, or couldn't stay with us... It was sad, and very hard. After a few months, I was able to help my "wife" get off the streets and into an apartment. It was a run-down, cockroach-infested one bedroom that she would share with a roommate in a rough part of town, but it was better than nothing. At the same time, my landlady was strongly suggesting that we move, because she never agreed to my daughter living there full-time, and my income was dropping along with my weight. Suddenly, I lost nearly forty pounds in just under four months. My usual sunny disposition wasn't so sunny, and my having the "patience of Job," well, that didn't apply anymore. I hardly recognized myself. I couldn't concentrate, and normal procedures and processes I would forget or screw up so badly, that I was getting in trouble at work with each deal.

Finally, one afternoon, a coworker asked me a question. A simple question, and my reaction was to grab him by the throat and force him against a wall and nearly choke him! I was pulled off of him, and immediately taken to my doctor's office. I had a complete meltdown. The stress of the last few years, hell, of a lifetime, had come to a head, and my mind had frozen. I don't know how else to describe it. The person I always knew to be me wasn't present and couldn't be found. Talk about feeling lost. When you don't recognize yourself, now that's scary. I was a familiar face in the mirror, but that spirit inside was hollow, shaken, completely unstable. The mind that had taken raw ideas and had transported them to creative realities couldn't even complete a simple thought, couldn't add two columns of numbers. My doctor ordered that I be put on disability, and that I see a psychiatrist immediately. The drugs he put me on made some things better, but most things worse. Within a four-month period—just over a hundred days—I went from being a functional member of society, although I had been on a slow downward trend, to nearly a babbling idiot. A babbling idiot with a daughter to care for, and one who had forgotten nearly everything in his past. Not just my past, but my short-term memory was gone, too. I was suddenly not recognizing my surroundings, wherever I was, becoming totally lost and frightfully confused.

This would happen many times during the day, no matter what I was doing or where I was. I could be driving and all of a sudden, I wouldn't know where I was or where I was going. If my daughter was with me, after we both got used to this, she'd say, "Calm down, Dad. We're two blocks from home or get off on the next exit." She was a great calming source, and a great navigator. My "fugue" episodes, as the doctors called them, scared the hell out of me. Thank God for my daughter and her cool head. She really did get me through this unbelievably difficult time. As I began to understand these "fugue episodes," I feared them less and would wait for them to pass, often missing a turnoff or address. I got lost a lot—I mean a lot! Actually, I still do. For that matter, I still have these "episodes," just not as frequently. And my memory, even now, is like a file drawer with files that are there sometimes; other times, not. It is so frustrating, to use an old line of my mother's: "I could just spit!"

My doctors had hoped that some time off of work would relieve the pressure that was causing my symptoms, but soon realized that was not the case, and declared me "permanently disabled." This meant little to me at the time; I was not really understanding what was happening. I was almost a zombie. Between whatever was going on in my mind and spirit combined with those goddamned drugs, I was punch-drunk all the time. If it wasn't for the exceptional care I received from my primary doctor, I think I would have fallen through the cracks and wound up another statistic— homeless and counted out by society.

But she cared. She must have known that she was my only lifeline. Without my knowledge, she called the psychiatrist she had referred me to. Knowing that my employer-based health insurance would expire now that I was permanently disabled, the two of them arranged, spending hours of their own time, for me to be accepted as an outpatient at a teaching clinic that didn't require insurance. This mission of mercy on both their parts most likely saved my life. The Gifford Clinic in San Diego became my weekly touchstone with reality. The interns would, under the kind supervision of the teaching doctors, assess my condition and progress (or lack thereof) and provide me, in a weird way, with a reason to exist. Mind you, I was never suicidal, even with a diagnosis of "chronic depression." For that matter, when they told me that my problem was "depression," I was surprised and told them that I was the happiest depressed guy you'd ever meet! And I still am! A small joke, because we know that's not how depression works.

When I was put on disability, my income dropped dramatically. I had little in savings, and my landlady was, especially with my new diagnosis, most eager to see us go. With the future looking bleak, and my financial future exceptionally insecure, I searched for the cheapest apartment out there. I found it, in the building directly across the courtyard from where my daughter's mother now lived—in the ghetto. Monthly rent of $715 for a one-bedroom cockroach-infested, gangbanger-run building in the City Heights neighborhood of San Diego. With no light at the end of the tunnel, with no pot of gold at the end of the rainbow—with no rainbow, I had little choice. I rented that run-down, dark apartment. This was all done in a fog. I was not thinking clearly at all. I did have the help of some people from work who were kind to me, who advised me, but I wasn't really present. I was just going through the motions. Because of my condition, because I wasn't thinking clearly, I thought that being close to her mother might be helpful. It was, at times. Mostly, being close to her just reminded both my daughter and me why we lived apart.

Living in this apartment and neighborhood was in many ways, like being in a foreign country. I had neighbors from Ethiopia and

Zimbabwe, Mexico and Haiti. These were wonderful, colorful people with great stories and love for their cultures and for the opportunities this country gave them. But my other neighbors were local gang members, Mexican Americans and Blacks who would fight in the alley behind our building at all hours, day or night, cops coming, lights flashing and sirens blaring. Between the gang members and the cockroaches and the police sirens, getting a full night's sleep was impossible.

I would walk my daughter to and from school each day. She made friends, as kids do, and seemed to be okay. Oddly, the local Mexican gangbangers took to me and nicknamed me "O.G.," short for Original Gangster! I accepted their friendship, and in return, received their protection. No one bothered us. It was funny, as if there was some sort of rumor milling around about me or something, because these bad dudes treated me with respect. I had some street smarts and knew not to question my good fortune. I just smiled and tipped my hat as my gangster buddies would nod to me or say hello. One time, not too long after moving to the "'hood," I was having breakfast alone at the local Denny's. A few of the local "bangers" gave me the nod as they left the restaurant, and the two cops who were just finishing their coffee came over and joined me in my booth. They were concerned that I was a new "supplier" in the area and thought that we should be on a first-name basis.

Man, did they ever read that wrong! I was just trying to keep my daughter and myself safe. When I told them that I somehow was regarded by the locals as an "O.G.," as someone to be treated with respect, and I wasn't going to dissuade them, they got the picture. By the end of my "coffee with the cops," they understood, and told me that they, too, would look out for us. It was a dangerous place. If I'd had the resources, mental, emotional, or financial, I would never had exposed us to such a toxic environment. But I didn't have them. I was doing the best I could, and it wasn't very good.

My days were spent in a mental fog. I'd watch TV, but not really. I'd sleep, but never feel rested. I had no appetite. My normal, healthy weight of 160 pounds was now down to 128 pounds. Each day the same. Empty space between taking care of my daughter. Thank God for her. If it weren't for her and having to care for her, I think I would have just faded away. At this time, there was nothing else. The time between caring for her and seeing someone at the clinic was a wasteland... dark, sad, empty, frustrating, and lonely. Something I'd never been. Lonely. I had few clear memories, which was so scary. I knew the memories were there and that I had done wonderful things with fabulous people. I had the photos, but I didn't remember, not really. The people in those pictures were gone or not close enough to disclose my current condition to! God forbid I break the unwritten law and show any weakness! I couldn't call them to fill in the details of my recent past. No, I felt very much alone, and for the first time in my life, lonely.

Having her mother nearby, who was on the wagon at this time, gave me the ability to visit my dear friends Rocco and Debbie Presutti in San Pedro. They were so wonderful to me through all of this. I would call them often, just to have someone to talk with. They were always patient with me, listening intently as I would try to finish a thought or try to get through a story—often tearfully because I would break down for little or no reason. During one of these calls, they invited me to come to their home, one I'd visited many times before. On my drive north from San Diego to my hometown of San Pedro, a drive I'd made a hundred times or more, I had to pull off the freeway three times to call Rocco for directions! Three times because I was lost on a freeway that, except for a couple of freeway changes, is a straight shot! I was a mess! When I finally arrived, I was met by my totally accepting and loving friends, Rocco and Debbie. That became the first of many weekends spent at their house. I'd sometimes sit in a rocking chair looking out over Los Angeles Harbor for hours as they went about their day. They just knew that I needed to be with them, even if I was silent for hours at a time (something I'd never done prior to getting sick!). When I did begin to engage in conversation, Rocco, who works with troubled vets at the V.A. and had experience in dealing with issues similar to mine, gently started introducing memories that we had shared together. We'd talk about "old times" with him filling in the blanks for me, and we usually ended up in hysterical laughter. We would go to places in San Pedro where we used to hang out, where I, or we, used to live, where this or that happened, in order to spark or solidify memories, and again, with Rocco's wild and wonderful sense of humor, make new ones.

And Debbie was right there, too.

From the moment I met her, some twenty-five years earlier, she had accepted me as Rocco's brother, and now, in my time of extreme need, she was right there. They were my contact with normalcy. They loved me. Even now. Broken. Broke. I'd be weeping, rocking in that chair and Debbie would say, "Let's go," and off we'd go, me along for the ride as she'd do her daily errands, making me feel... just a little normal. May not sound like much, but it was the world. Man was it ever! To be out and about like regular folks was a win for me—it was big. And being there with them allowed me to relax. I didn't have to care for my daughter, not that I minded, but in my condition at that time, caring for her was all consuming and left little energy for my recovery. It also let me see, once again, how "normal" people live. They're not falling-down drunk! They don't live in cockroach-infested homes surrounded by gangbangers fighting outside their door day and night. I was so numb to my surroundings that, had I not had those visits with Rocco and Deb, I may have forgotten what decent society looked like—and may have never stoked the small spark of hope that Rocco gave me.

When I was diagnosed with "chronic depression" and granted permanent disability, it was again something that, in my condition, I didn't quite understand the ramifications of. It was suggested that I retain a lawyer, and not being of sound mind, I contacted a law firm that advertised on television that Social Security Disability was their specialty. I signed up and followed their instructions and waited. I was told that it could take as long as two to three years before my case was heard, and that I should be patient, because my case would surely have a positive outcome.

Providing that I stayed unemployed.

Wait! What? Two to three years before my case is heard, but my unemployment insurance payments from the State of California were going to run out in just a few months, and I had no savings! How was I going to keep a roof over our heads and food on the table while I waited for a trial date? The "lawyer" told me to beg or borrow, but if I went to work doing ANYTHING, my case was lost, over, and they would drop me as a client! I didn't know what to do.

There was no way I could get from here to there, even if I lucked out and got the earliest court date possible. Stress like this would shut me down. I'd just sit and rock for hours, not really doing or thinking, just rocking, rocking. I had nowhere to go for that kind of money. I had to get a job. I was in no kind of shape to do even the simplest of tasks, but the bills kept coming and I had to do something. The agreement with the attorney clearly stated that if I became employed, even part time, I was obligated to inform them. It also said that any type of employment would severely damage my case, if not cause it to be thrown out altogether. The prospect of losing my permanent disability added to the terrible suffering I was experiencing from my illness. Without the lifeline that social security would provide, I feared I couldn't provide even the basic necessities for my daughter and myself.

Rocco, being a musician as well as a mental health counselor, came up with a simple plan to help me recapture cognitive skills and short-term memory. He told me to buy a "real book" and study the songs. Real books are books of sheet music with the lyrics of songs regarded as "standards." These were the songs that I had performed hundreds of times back in the day. He suggested that I play my CD's while I read the music and sang along, engaging as many of my senses as possible. I did this very pleasurable exercise hour after hour, reading the songs as I sang along, old favorite after another. It felt great to sing again. Slowly, and I mean very slowly, I was able to look away from the sheet music and sing the words from memory, first a few lines, then a few more. The progress was gradual, but it didn't go unnoticed. My daughter clapped like a crazed fan the first time I sang a song all the way through without having to read the lyrics. It wasn't a small thing. Not to us. I called Rocco and Debbie so that we could celebrate that milestone together.

That milestone was hope. Suddenly, I had hope. Hope that I could recapture my ability to recall things. Hope that I could get better. And,

I could sing. I had all but forgotten that I had this talent, this gift. I had forgotten nearly everything that I had ever done. But if I can remember the words to a song, maybe I can remember the words to two songs! I started to sing songs day and night, reading from my real book while I listened to the song on CD, then writing the lyrics. I was relentless. A few things happened: I began to feel more secure with myself; my voice started to come back (it had been years since I'd sung); and I fell in love with the music again.

Once again, music had given my life purpose.

The financial problems mounted when my final State disability check was on the horizon. One last attempt for leniency from the attorney failed; work and we'll drop you, they told me, but I had no choice. Rocco's exercise did more than tune up my voice, it gave me a bit of confidence, enough to approach my old friend Jeff Gerken. Jeff had hired me many years earlier at the BMW dealership he still managed in El Cajon, about 15 miles east of San Diego. We had stayed in touch over the years. He had enjoyed knowing that I left his employment and went on to produce big-name shows. Whenever we spoke, he always made a point of saying that he often told stories about me to employees and customers alike! Well, swallowing my pride, I stopped in to see him, and when I told him of my situation, and of my illness and disability, he smiled and joked that "…you were always fucked-up, and that's why I like you. You're hired!"

What a great guy. I was completely honest about my limitations. He said he'd do his best to help me, and if I was as messed up as I said I was, he'd still keep me as long as he could. Our goal was to get to the social security hearing date, which was not yet set. He put up with me for nine months, God bless him. That was a complete act of kindness. Selling high-line automobiles requires in-depth product knowledge and professional customer-relation skills, neither of which I possessed. I was more like a guy on his first day of work—every day! I couldn't remember what to do, when to do it, where to put it, who to give it to…. I was shot! Jeff covered my butt for nine months because he knew what was at stake for his old pal. But Jeff had a boss to answer to who wasn't very interested in my sad tale. So, when he could no longer carry me, he called me into his office and told me the ride was over. But, he had arranged for me to work for a friend of his at a Nissan dealership. He had explained my situation to his friend, who was happy to help. Once again, someone was watching over me. This time, it was my old pal Jeff!

Through this period, whenever I was at home, I was singing like crazy in my little apartment, entertaining the neighbors and all of our cockroaches. The job at the Nissan store was nice and laid back. That was okay with me. I was just praying that I could do my job, which was so very hard. Even then, with nearly two years of weekly counseling and different medications, I still would get lost constantly and have "fugue" episodes. My level of concentration was that of a five-year-old, causing all kinds of delays to processes, making simple tasks confusing. And although I was the recipient of great kindness, the stress of knowing that I couldn't do the simplest of tasks without assistance was wearing on me, causing me to backslide. My memory, for what it was worth, was getting worse. And again, I had no appetite.

I worried that my new employer wouldn't have Jeff's patience. Four months into my new job, my performance review wasn't too pretty. So, to release the stress, when I got home, I'd sing!

In this photo, I am talking with Rocco and Deb Presutti at their home in San Pedro. We've been like family since the moment we met more than 40 years ago.

Chapter 16

FULL CIRCLE

"How's the singing coming?" Rocco asked. I had called him to tell him that I finally received the notice for my court date. He was concerned for me because his experience with mental health issues led him to believe that cases like mine rarely were awarded permanent disability social security benefits. The fact that my attorney had dropped me as a client because I had returned to work seemed to further support his position, and he now had me worried. My employment at the Nissan dealership wasn't going to last much longer, I knew that. And beyond that, I didn't know where I'd turn. But for now, with this job I had enough income to cover our needs if I could just hold out for a few more months....

"Rocco, the singing's great! And I think I'm getting pretty good. But you know what's happened? I've fallen in love with the music again. I love these songs, the stories they tell, the way they tell them."

"So why don't you start performing again?"

"Oh, no. I couldn't. I'm nowhere near ready for that!" I said.

Rocco put an ad on Craigslist for me: "Old Style Crooner Available." The very day the ad posted I got a call from a guitarist who had a jazz trio that wanted to be a quartet. That guitarist was Rick Ross. Rick would hold rehearsal each Wednesday at 1:30 in his home, and that next Wednesday, I was there. I was scared to death. Funny, really. Driving to Rick's, which was a forty-five-minute drive without getting lost, I had to talk myself into continuing on... I was actually sweating. I was a nervous wreck. Here I was, a guy who had done hundreds of shows myself, produced hundreds more, and I was shaking in my boots over an audition! But I went, and that was a victory. And I sang. Not so well by my standards, but good enough for Rick to see that with some rehearsals, I could do the job.

I was in! I was part of a band again. I was so proud, I could have burst. I can't convey how important this was—how validating it was. To belong to something; to be appreciated and valued by quality musicians, now that was something to build on. I may have trouble finding my way back home, but I was in a band. And with good players, too. Guitar, electric bass, and drums. They had been working out together for a while and were pretty tight. Nice guys, all retired, just playing music for fun, basically.

Rick had given me a list of songs to learn for the follow week's rehearsal. I had something to do, something that was targeted, that was for a specific reason. I was in a band! The moment I got home I called Rocco to share the news, so excited to tell him how his pushing me to get the real book and to practice the songs had actually led to my being in a band again, but he wasn't there and so my call went to voicemail. Damn, I wanted to tell him so badly. I knew that I had accomplished something here, for me, something big. During this time, I rarely ventured outside of the apartment to socialize. When I could, I'd visit Rocco and Deb. I had a pal from the Lexus store I'd occasionally see, but that was it. I was too shaky. My ability to concentrate and carry on a conversion of any depth didn't exist, and I was painfully aware of my shortcomings. A once highly socialized creature, I was now reclusive and insecure. I couldn't remember which TV show I just watched, let alone keep up with a snappy conversation. So, for me to venture out and audition for this singing gig was HUGE, and I was bursting to tell Rocco about it! God damn it, Roc! Where are you? ...

And then the phone rang. "Hey, mongoose, what's up?"

Mongoose. Don't ask, 'cause I don't know. Hell, he doesn't know, or remember, either, but that's the nickname Rocco hung on me back when we were teenagers.

"I got the gig!" I told him as I started to cry. "They liked me, Roc. I rehearse every Wednesday," I choked out. I had to stop. I was crying too hard to talk, to thank him. He was used to this. I did this a lot. Hell, I still do. But this time the tears were happy ones, not sad or confused tears, but grateful, hopeful and happy tears, and Rocco was soaking in the moment with me. He knew that it was a victory that wouldn't have been won without him, but he never looked for credit, ever. Whenever I tried to give him credit, he would turn it back on me, saying that it was me who did the work, did the exercises. But he deserved credit. And a lot of it. So, does Deb.

I love them. They are my family.

My boss at the Nissan store called me in to discuss my future with the company. Knowing my situation, he had been extremely patient with me. However, he had a boss to answer to as well, and was starting to get some heat because of my poor sales numbers. I let him know that I had my court date soon, and if he could keep me on in any capacity for a few more months, it would mean the world to my daughter and me.

"Oh, and by the way, can I have Wednesday afternoons off? I have band rehearsal."

"You've got balls!" was his reply. And with a shake of his head, he chuckled and told me, "Sure, why not." We both knew I wasn't long for the place, so really, what was the difference? He told me if anyone asked, I had a standing doctor's appointment. It was therapy, after all.

With my court date approaching, I contacted the law firm, hoping that they would reverse their position and represent me in court. They wouldn't. They pretty much convinced me that even my going to the hearing was a waste of time. Pretty much. But on the night before my hearing, I decided to go. The next morning, I left very early, allowing lots of time to get lost. I got there early and walked into an empty courtroom.

Or so I thought.

The gallery was empty, but behind a raised podium a man was on the phone. As I sat, he covered the mouthpiece and asked who I was. I told him, and he said that he was the judge overseeing my case and that he was on the phone with the psychiatrist who was reviewing my file, and that he'd be right with me. Almost as a reflex, he then re-covered the phone and asked me where my attorney was. I told him that they were not coming. He asked why, and I told him that I had to go back to work to support my daughter and myself, so they dropped me because they said that I would lose the case. He held up his hand to me, to have me stop speaking for a moment as he again spoke to the doctor briefly on the phone, then hung up and turned his full attention to me.

His friendly attitude had become stern as he expressed his disdain for this law firm, and then he said to me, "Relax, Mr. Marin. The doctor and I have reviewed your case and we agree that you are entitled to full disability benefits. What's more, I will read into the instructions that your attorney will have no claim to any portion of your award should they try to collect. Relax, Mr. Marin. From what I've seen here, you have been through enough. Court will be in session in a few minutes and I will make this official. I am truly sorry for the way that law firm treated you and wish you all the best."

And with that, a tremendous weight was lifted from my shoulders. I was told that I would receive a monthly check for the rest of my life, and back pay to the day I was originally disabled, nearly three years earlier. Once again, someone was watching over me, because according to Rocco and the television law firm and so many armchair experts I'd spoken with, I'd beaten the odds—some very long odds— and won my case. Thank God. And thank you, your Honor. You changed, and probably saved, our lives.

The trio had now made me an official member, and after a couple of months of Wednesday rehearsals, Rick announced a name change, 'cause we weren't a trio anymore. He named us "JazzClub." Rick gave us the business cards that he'd had made; now we were official! He also said that we would make our first public appearance. He'd booked us at a popular beach-side restaurant and bar that was famous for its sunset views: the Beachhouse, in Cardiff, about fifteen miles north of San Diego. "Call your friends and family, because we want to make a good showing," he said.

And so, it began. I was back in the saddle again, but just the thought of standing in front of an audience, singing songs from memory, scared the hell out of me, so much so that I nearly quit the band, the newly minted JazzClub. I hung back after rehearsal to let Rick know of my reservations. My days as a young singer, decades earlier required a level of performance that wasn't being called for here, but that wasn't my point of reference. I was basing my ability to deliver and perform on that former degree of professionalism. I was not up to speed. They were, but my voice, although improving, I knew, was not where it could be. Plus, I was insecure because of my memory.

Rick assured me that it would be fine if I kept my music on a music stand and referenced the music and words, but to me, this was so unprofessional. To the "old me," it was, and that was what I had to get used to. The "old me" could remember the lyrics to hundreds of songs and do requests all night long. Now, I had to come to terms with having a music stand on stage because I couldn't recall the lyrics to, or trust myself to recall, just a few songs. Rick, in his inimitable fashion, said not to worry. "The Beachhouse is a shitbox," he said. "All these joints are just shitboxes. Don't worry about it. You're gonna blow these know-nothing, overweight, drunk slobs away," he said as he laughed. "You'll be great!" I didn't share Rick's enthusiasm, but I appreciated his confidence. "Hey, maybe you'll meet a nice girl!" he added. Being the perfect Jewish mother at times, and a wonderful friend all the time, he was looking out for my happiness. Rick was right. We blew them away, and the club booked us for months out. But

I didn't meet a nice girl. I wasn't looking. In fact, I wanted nothing to do with "girls" of any kind. I was in no shape to be in a relationship. Plus, my history in this area wasn't so good. No, I was gun-shy when it came to this subject, to say the least!

But the music had me so excited. JazzClub was soon getting booked into clubs and restaurants all over the place! We were playing two and three nights a week, rehearsing every Wednesday afternoon, and very quickly growing our repertoire and if I say so myself, getting pretty damn good. At home, I would practice as much as possible, hoping that this would completely ward off the symptoms of my illness, but it didn't. Yet the music gave me hope. It had already given me a new lease on life, and through my frustration, I would have to remind myself of that. When I would get lost, I would sing. When I would forget what I was saying, mid-sentence, I would take a deep breath and think of the music and relax. Music was my safe place now, even when I was with others, I would listen silently in my head to it until it calmed me, until I was back in the present.

It was difficult holding the job down at the Nissan store. I would mix up the order of things, slowing down the sales and delivery procedures, making the lives of the other employees just a bit more difficult. I was well liked by the staff, which helped with my being tolerated for my shortcomings, but the time had come for us to part. As I arrived for an afternoon shift, my boss uttered those dreaded words: "Peter, have you got a minute?" I wanted to beg for another month or two of work, doing anything, because I was at least that far away from getting my social security check, but I knew it wouldn't matter. I was grateful for them doing all that they had done for me. He handed me my final check. After saying goodbye to my coworkers, I got in my car and opened the envelope to look at my check. It might get us through the next two or three weeks, if I hold the strings real tight.

The gigs with JazzClub brought in $75 to $100 each, plus maybe $20 or $30 in tips, nothing to write home about, but it helped. The final check from work was gone all too soon, and the gig money kept us in cheap groceries and gas, but trouble was everywhere. I couldn't see how I could pay the rent, low as it was, and still provide food and the other necessities my daughter and I needed. I was sick with worry. I tried to find work of any kind to patch us through, but nothing. I kept thinking that if only we can stay afloat for two more months, we'd be fine, but two months without income is a long time. It came down to pay the rent or eat, so we ate. I felt horrible about this, so I called the slumlord who owned the building and explained my circumstances. I offered to give them a lien on my settlement, assuring them of my intention to pay. They instead responded with a pay or quit notice, which of course I could not do, which then led to an eviction notice.

Desperate not to be homeless, I swallowed my pride and called a new friend I had made while working at the Lexus dealership. Bill, whose last name I'll leave out as not to embarrass him, bought a car from me. In the process, we found out that we had lots in common. His son was marrying a girl from San Pedro, who happened to be the niece of a gal I once knew. With that common thread, we became pals and started to have lunch now and then. When I got sick, Bill would call and check on me from time to time, and when I started to sing again, he and his wife, Rosie, were my biggest supporters. I knew they were very wealthy, the kind of wealth that goes a generation or two deep, but that didn't make my asking any easier (maybe harder, actually), but I saw no other option. The call I made to Bill was one of the most difficult calls I've ever made. Asking for help shouldn't be so hard.

Why did I feel like such a failure? Was it the stigma of mental illness? Or was it the rawness of need, of being desperate that stripped me of dignity and self-worth? Recalling what my old friend Jack Millman would say, "You can't eat pride, and it won't pay your bills," I swallowed mine and made the call.

Bill listened patiently as I explained my situation and said that he would discuss it with Rosie and get back to me. He called back within an hour, knowing I was probably pacing the floor, to give me the location of the bank where we could meet in the morning. I can't tell you how relieved and grateful I felt at that moment. So many emotions washed over me. To be so dependent on others was something I couldn't get used to and certainly wasn't comfortable with, and to receive such kindness and generosity was overwhelming. Realizing that with this loan from Bill and Rosie, my daughter and I would survive at least the financial side of the nightmare we'd been living, as I ended the call with Bill, I put my head in my hands and cried and cried... tears of relief.

When I met Bill at the bank the next morning, he handed me an envelope with cash and said that they don't loan money. This was a gift. Plus, there was more money in the envelope than I had asked for. This was such a great kindness. God bless them. Still, after all these years, if they're in town, they come to my performances and always stuff the tip jar. But money aside, these are two of the sweetest people I've ever met, and, I'm so happy to have them as friends.

We moved out of that horrible apartment as soon as my back pay from my disability benefits arrived. Point Loma (just west of San Diego) had good schools for my daughter, beautiful neighborhoods, shopping centers, and not a gangbanger in sight! The apartment we took was more expensive than I could afford, but with my singing income and my social security, we'd squeak by. The tree-lined, pristine walkways that meandered throughout this beautiful complex with pools and tennis courts was so far from the cockroach motel atmosphere we were used to that I didn't care what it cost, I wanted to live there. I wanted us to experience again what it was like to have self-respect and be around people who cared about themselves and their surroundings. Yes, it was twice what I had been paying in that ghetto apartment, and yes, more than I should be paying, but it was like water to a thirsty man. I couldn't move us in fast enough. This beautiful environment was so peaceful by comparison, it was like night and day. The constant thought that danger was near with each trip to the store or to my daughter's school was replaced with... nothing. No fear. It was palpable.

The screaming from a neighbor's apartment was replaced by the sounds of tennis balls pinging off of rackets echoing through the quiet complex. Our lives had changed dramatically, and I was so appreciative. Piece by piece, I was clawing my way back to the surface. That's what all this felt like. It was like being submerged. For years now, throughout the psychological treatment, the various drugs that had been tried to treat my issues, it felt as if I was somehow under.... something, water, I don't know, something. Never quite on top of anything. I was late to the party, slow to get the drift of things, and always forgetful. Embarrassingly so. I had become this new person, this alternate me who was a shell of the former inhabitant. This version who no longer could trust myself to engage in conversations for fear of losing track and embarrassing myself. This version who withdrew from social contact, except that that came with the gigs.

Time allowed me to become adjusted to the effects of my illness, such as the "fugue" events, and I developed coping methods to get me through. If it weren't for the music, for my singing, I'm afraid I wouldn't have been able to swim up to anywhere near the surface again. At that point, on my best days, when recalling a memory or engaged in a conversation, I felt like I was walking on a thinly frozen lake, just waiting for the ice to crack beneath me, leaving my mind blank, frozen, completely unaware of what was being discussed, and me, embarrassed.

It was these feelings of inadequacy, combined with my poor history with women, that kept me from dating. Rick was always after me to find a nice girl. At the gigs, women were everywhere, and after a while, the guys in the band started teasing me, figuring I had to be gay, not that there's anything wrong with that, as Seinfeld said. But I had no desire. None. You see, I remembered what I used to be like, who I used to be. It's not like I didn't know. I knew what I had accomplished, who I had associated with, worked and played with. Until I had something to offer someone, something of value, I wasn't interested. Who would want to be with me, this burned-out guy struggling to make ends meet and hoping to remember his way home from the market? No, I wasn't ready. But I was determined to get better, and the best thing that gave me results was the music, so I dove more deeply into it. Whenever I could I'd sit in with other bands or visit jam sessions around town, getting to know the players. Before long, I was getting calls to work with groups or players outside of JazzClub. I was making a local name for myself.

All of this activity had gotten my voice in the best shape it had been in in years, and when it came to singing, I had my confidence back. It felt good—no, great—to know that there was something I could do, some way that I could contribute to our lives. Not too long before, I had all but resigned myself to a life of rocking side to side in a dimly lit room, hour after hour, staring blankly at the TV or out the window... that was my life when I started singing in that cockroach-infested apartment. Now, when I walked into a club, musicians called my name and welcomed me to the stage, fans offering a seat or to buy me a drink.

There, I had value. In spite of my mental limitations, I could sing, and that's all they cared about. I was welcome in their community. It felt really nice to fit in. Although I still needed to read my music on stage, no one seemed to mind. And if I got lost going to the gig, nobody knew, because I always left early enough to allow for it. I had found ways to overcome my shortcomings, like never getting involved in long conversations, keeping everything light and on the surface, Mr. Happy-Go-Lucky. And I was, for the most part, happy. I had come to grips with the changes in me. I accepted that my memory would forever be unreliable at best, and the guy who used to run million-dollar concerts with notes on a clipboard was gone. I was encouraged because music had made me viable again, made me a participant in life again. So, what if I couldn't add two columns of numbers together, they have calculators for that! And so what if I get lost? I'll just have to make enough money singing to get off of social security disability and buy a car with navigation! This modern world has devices to help a brain like mine; all it takes is money. I made it before, why not now?

By this point, I was off of the medications completely. The antidepressants I had been given over the years never seemed to accomplish what the doctors had hoped, and one had given me a lung infection that was so serious and frightening that I thought I had lung cancer. After that experience, I wanted nothing to do with those medications, so, with the doctor's help, I was weaned off all of the drugs. My doctor was tempted to try Adderall, but with my prior history of speed usage, which he and other doctors described as "self-medicating" (can you believe that?), we decided against it. Being without the antidepressants, I began to feel again, to experience more acutely emotions. Without realizing it, the last few years had been spent in emotional neutral. These drugs left me floating in limbo, not really too happy or sad, taking the edge off of everything. Now, as I saw things more as they really were, I found myself reacting to the smallest things.

Or more like it, overreacting. It wasn't as if I was manic, but I'd find myself in tears while watching a TV commercial, for Christ sakes. It's well known that the Italians are a bit emotional but come on! I was as raw as a baby. I'd catch myself starting to weep while listening to someone describe a sad situation or even while singing a touching love song... my filters were down. I was processing emotions more honestly than ever, and once I realized this, I was no longer embarrassed by my tears.

I began to understand that this change given to me through my illness was a gift. To process feelings so cleanly and without the prejudices that my former mind would put them through took time for me to get used to. Others, I came to realize, didn't so easily understand. Tears make people uncomfortable, especially from a man. I'd explain, time and again, that I was fine, as someone would fawn over me when I started to leak as they told a story that touched me. And, not wanting to share my history with everyone, I was often viewed as strange, I'm sure. Well, I am. With time, some filters came have come back, but just some. I still cry at commercials and while singing songs with great stories to tell, be it happy or sad, but now I wear those tears as a badge of honor.

Permanently disabled. This is my new label. I don't like it. There's a lot of good that it does for me, and for others I'm sure, but me, I just don't like it. The handle implies that I am less than, that I am unable to compete or contribute in ALL segments of life. I believed it, too, when all of this began, before I found something to devote myself to. Of course, that something for me was and is singing, but I believe that the process I went through may apply for many people suffering from depression or other forms of mental illness.

My theory is simple. Find something that turns you on, something that you are passionate about. I don't care if it's sewing or growing flowers, writing poems or making music, anything that consumes you and allows you to create something that you can share with others. I think this is the key, these two elements.

First, in losing yourself to a creative process, you release whatever is troubling you, bringing much needed, albeit temporary, relief. After a while, you may notice that this "exercise" of sewing or writing or gardening is more than just a distraction, because it is something that allows you to contribute to your family and friends, making you an active participant in life. And this I feel is key, that whatever you do, you share it. Me, I sing my songs to whoever will listen. This gives me great joy, to be able to share my voice and my "gift." If I had continued to sing in my dark little apartment and never ventured out to share my passion, I would not have progressed as a singer, but much more importantly, I would not have found a viable position in society. I would have laid down and given up and spent the rest of my life believing and living like I was PERMANENTLY DISABLED.

True, I am disabled. I can no longer manage things as I once did. If it weren't for singing, I don't know what I would have done to heal, or to supplement my disability income. In stressful situations, my mind shuts down, making recall nearly impossible. I could not hold down a nine to five. I'd drive a boss nuts with all my forgetting, and the insecurity that it would create in me would be devastating. I'm lucky to have my background in music, and with my re-born "career," I set out to change my label of "permanently disabled." I wanted to get off of the monthly disability checks and earn my own way.

I learned as a kid hustling deals in Hollywood that the better the company you kept, the better chance you had to make things happen. Applying this theory to my singing, I sought out the best musicians in San Diego and Los Angeles to work with. I soon had a little black book of phone numbers connecting me to the finest players around, which, according to my theory, would result in doing my best work with the finest players in the best venues for the most money. Well, most of that worked out. The gig scene, as it turned out, pay wise, really hasn't changed much over the years. Local clubs and restaurants were still paying next to nothing, and even though I had earned the respect of some of Southern California's finest jazz musicians, to take home $150 per night, tips included, made for a poor business model. The "casual gig" market, where one could make a decent living—private parties, weddings, and corporate events generally went to dance bands, although I did get calls occasionally, but not enough to count on.

My desire to make a living as a working musician and to get off of disability would take more than singing in local clubs. Unless, of course, I listened to the voice of my old manager Paul Henderson, still fresh in my head after all these years pleading with me to sing "Top 40 dance tunes"; I couldn't do it then, I still couldn't decades later! Unlike so many musicians, I don't teach music or singing, which is a common income source for musicians. I don't, because I don't have the formal education, and therefore don't feel qualified.

Yet I had to find a way up from the bottom rung of this ladder.

One night while playing at a club with my pal Rick Ross, he introduced me to a friend of his, Mark Shapiro. Mark is a world-class guitarist and producer, and someone I'd heard of because of his work with the great smooth jazz group Fattburger. We became fast friends, and before long, Mark educated me on the merits of having a recording of my work. At the very least, I should have a demo CD, even a live recording, something to put on the Internet and to leave behind after a sales call. This, along with a decent webpage, would be a good place to start my climb up that ladder. I called an old friend from San Pedro, the third wheel who hung out with Rocco and me during our misspent youth, Frank Unzueta. Frank's a great pianist and arranger who I sang a lot with as a kid. We discussed doing a CD, something simple, inexpensive but good. I picked out the songs and sent them to Frank, so he could write the arrangements for a trio: piano, bass, and drums (classic jazz piano trio setup). On the day of the recording session, Mark, my daughter, and I drove to L.A. and met the players at the studio. They were all top studio guys in town: Larry Steen on bass and, as it turned out, Frank had contracted Gordon Peeke to play drums, whom I had known from many years before!

It was great having old friends on the project, and that morning the music just flowed as smooth as glass. The arrangements that Frank wrote were so strong, and the studio performances so good, that once Mark and I got them back to his studio near San Diego, we knew that we had to expand the project. Our plan was to record the trio parts in Los Angeles and then record my vocals in his studio, where we would also later do the final mix and master. This would allow us to take our time recording my vocals and control costs. Now that we had these world-class, broadcast-worthy instrumental tracks, which were way beyond what we had envisioned, our focused changed. What had been a project to produce a giveaway demo CD had morphed into a serious endeavor, or at least one that had that potential. We started recording my vocals, and with Mark's deft producing skill, he got everything there was to get out of me. But I had something else at my disposal that I didn't want to get away— Mark's skill as a guitarist. I asked, and he responded by adding the cream that the CD needed! This once simple and cheap demo project that was originally meant to be no more than a fancy calling card was now ready for worldwide release. It was that good, if I say so myself! One day, as we were mixing a song, a man walked in Mark's studio. He quietly slipped in the door and leaned against it as it closed and just listened as we finished.

When we were done, this fellow said, "Working with the 'A' team on this project huh, Mark?" I secretly swelled with pride, of course, but was really proud when I was introduced to him, because this was a man who knew what he was talking about. Turns out he is not only a four-time Grammy winner and sitting member on the Grammy board of governors, and president of his own successful production and management company in New York, but he is also the son of one of the greatest singers and band leaders of all time. His name is Guy Eckstine, son of "Mr. B.," Billy Eckstine. Guy not only tells us that we should go to the top with this project, but he offers any assistance he can give! We immediately take him up on his offer and have him record the drum parts on "Angel Eyes." You see, on top of everything else, Guy is also a great drummer! Now, I've got him on the CD, and I'm starting to see some daylight for my plan. "Lay down with golden dogs and you get up with golden fleas," Jack Millman was fond of saying. These old saying have truth in them.

When I started singing again, I was really lucky to hook up with Rick Ross. Rick, although he insists that he only plays for fun, is a first-class musician, and more importantly, a first-class human being. With Rick at the center of my musical universe, he introduced me to not just the San Diego gig scene, but to the best players. He believed in me and worked with me to get me back in shape, both vocally and mentally. The introduction to Mark Shapiro was no accident. That didn't happen until Rick felt that I was ready, and when he thought that I was, he invited Mark to hear me perform, unbeknownst to me. Step by step, and with the support of my friends, my circle was growing. The tools in my toolbox, my repertoire, publicity pictures, website, connections (both with musicians and those on the business side of music), and now my CD, were not just growing, but were top quality. People who really could help advance my career, like Guy Eckstine, and my dear friend Rick Marcelli, were offering to do just that once we released my CD. So, in anticipation of chart-busting sales (wink wink), I penned an original song, a tongue-in-cheek autobiographical peek at my illustrious career titled "Overnight Success!" This became the title of the CD as well.

This was such an exciting time. Every day was focused on getting radio stations to play my CD, and to getting better local gigs. I began a marketing campaign by sending my CD to many radio stations across the country. The one station I was hoping to get was right here at home. The jazz station in San Diego, Jazz 88.3, is among the world's top-rated jazz stations, with Internet listenership worldwide, so when they agreed to put my CD in their rotation, I was thrilled! I can't describe the feeling I had when I heard myself on the radio for the first time. My daughter and I were driving when all of a sudden, the disc jockey gave a lead-in about a new CD from a popular local singer... he gave me a huge buildup, it was unbelievable, and then the music started.

My music.

We pulled over and just listened. Of course, I cried, like always. I am one leaking machine, but this was a moment like no other. One to treasure.

I had, no, we had, my daughter and I, had made it this far. And this was a long way from where our journey had begun. But there was more to do, a lot more if I was going to support us without the government's help. The way I had it figured, I needed to earn three times what my disability payments equaled, at a minimum, and in a manner that was sustainable. Club gigs alone, at the income level I was on, would not cut it. A few months prior to this, with Rick Ross' help, the band had started entertaining at retirement homes. His mother lived in an upscale retirement community that had three separate housing areas, and before long, we were performing there three to four times per month. Because this was daytime work and didn't compete with club gigs, I saw this as an opportunity to increase substantially the income I could create from live performances. Before long, we were playing on average three club gigs and three retirement home gigs per week. With the addition of the daylight-hour income effectively doubling my gigging revenue, I still wasn't close to my goal of earning three times my base. But there was light at the end of the tunnel.

My CD was making some noise locally. Jazz 88.3 kept playing my music, and even invited me to the studio for a live interview. Things were moving. My shows were full after that interview for six months, making the club owners happy and quick to rebook me. The local music papers wrote about me, little stuff, but I was out there, making noise, moving up that ladder, step by step. The reaction to my CD and my live shows was so positive, I was brave enough to reach out to some friends and acquaintances from my old days in show business. Before long, talks were underway with serious business management and talent agencies based in Los Angeles and New York. There were ideas of touring Japan and Germany and even recording another CD. Although my background taught me that these are the things of dreams, I still got caught up in the excitement of it. Of course, if any piece of this came true, my plan of supporting us unaided would become a reality. Just one more piece of the puzzle.

Right:

Having fun with "The Queen" Barbara Morrison, following her show that I served as Master of Ceremonies on. We both came up as young singers in Los Angeles. I would see her anytime I could, then and now. You see, there's a reason they call her "The Queen".

Below:

Here I am with the love of my life, Kim.

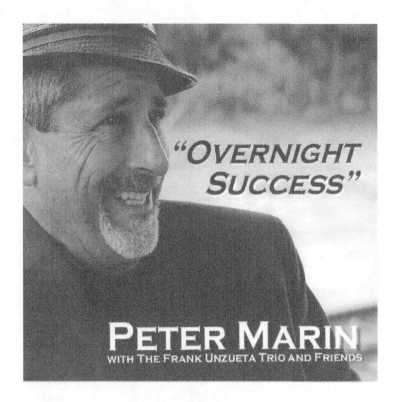

This is my CD cover from my 2012 recording. This truly marked a
milestone in my re-entry into society.

Chapter 17

A NEW PLAN

One hot, sunny summer afternoon, July 5, 2013, I had that puzzle piece in my pocket as I arrived at my gig at a nice hotel in San Diego. It was a steady gig, every Friday evening, poolside, May through September. This was my second year at this hotel, but this day, I had a new bass player who didn't know where to park. I walked across the parking lot to wave to her to get her attention.

And then it happened.

Somehow, water and a light sheet of mud had settled on a small rise in the cement. In the bright sunlight, I didn't see the mud or the slight hump in the asphalt. And I slipped, falling and twisting in a way that caused immense and immediate neck and back pain. As I collected myself, the spasms in my back, bad as they were, took a back seat to whatever was going on in my neck. I could not lift or turn my head. I knew that this was bad, really bad.

Bad. That was an understatement. The MRI showed that I had nerves jammed in where they shouldn't be, which explained why my chiropractor couldn't relieve my pain or increase my range of motion. For weeks I had been suffering with horrific pain from this stupid little slip. No big accident with sirens blaring, just a little fall seen only by my drummer. A tiny misstep, almost like those most of us take on any given day... almost.

Like the old saying says, "The show must go on," and so did my shows, in spite of the pain. My bandmates would help me with my sound equipment, because it hurt too much for me to lift it, and I'd sing either sitting on or leaning against a stool, to limit my movements. And as painful as this was, it didn't seem to hurt as much as the reality that now, with my needing major surgery and the requisite recovery, those agents and managers who were breathing heavily before were now gone.

Yup, that train had left the station.

"Hey, give us a call when you recover," or "Send us a copy of your next CD" were now the way they said their polite goodbyes. I understood. I didn't like it, but I got it. It takes stamina to perform. To tour, it takes good health, fitness, and stamina, and at the moment, I didn't qualify. I got it. But I was more than disappointed. I had been so close to moving up another rung or two on that ladder. One thing became clear: I needed a new puzzle piece. I'd crushed this one in my fall.

In the five years or so since I'd been a single father, I chose not to date for many reasons. I initially had my hands full taking care of my daughter, then, when I got sick and all that that entailed, well, as you read previously, I didn't regard myself as much of a prize. And let's not forget my history here— my last two long-term relationships were disasters! No, even though my bandmates and friends were always on the lookout for a nice woman for me, I was content being alone. I did have companionship, one friend, a very sweet and pretty woman whom I sold a Lexus to, would meet me for dinner and a movie regularly, but it was just a friendship. Another woman I met while shopping one morning invited me to her home once or twice a month. We never went out or even talked very much. We both just needed to have someone to touch, to hold.

This was enough for me at the time. I was grateful to have both "friends," who were kind and wonderful with me during a time when I was socially insecure. My daughter knew my "dinner and a movie" friend and didn't care much for her. Thinking I was ready for the dating scene and hoping to get me away from "Miss dinner and a movie," she and her best friend tried to set me up with her best friend's mother. Her mother and I both thought it was sweet, but we agreed that it was not a good idea. Yet the energy seemed to be silently flowing in the direction of romance... even if I was the last to realize it.

Rick Ross, from whom all good things had come lately, pointed out a wonderful woman who he felt would be perfect for me, named Kim. She was the activities director at the retirement community where we played many times a month. I describe her as wonderful, even though at this time I barely knew her, because of the way she interacted with the older folks she cared for. With them all in wheelchairs, she would dance with some, arms swinging, sing with others, or just hold a hand or stroke an arm while we played our music. Her joy in doing this was unrestrained and her love for her charges very real. I was so touched the first time I saw this that every time since, I paid special attention to her, even though Rick and Kim didn't realize it. When Kim and I first met, and Rick initially suggested I ask her out, I wasn't looking at her with romantic eyes. That's exactly what I had been resisting for years! Yet as I watched her while she moved around the room, talking and gently touching, laughing or consoling her aging crew, I could see how much she loved them and them her. She was something special. Someone special. And Rick, God love him, gave me not-so-gentle reminders all the time that I should pursue her.

One September morning as we finished our performance, Kim hired us to play for the New Year's Eve party. Because retirement community parties end at 7:00 pm, Rick, in his inimitable fashion, said "Hey, Kim, are you busy New Year's Eve?"

"Not after the party, Rick. Why?"

Rick then said, "Peter, do you have a date for New Years?"

"You know I don't, Rick!" I answer.

And we all just laughed it off... but a few minutes later, as I was driving home, as if being hit by lightning, I picked up my phone and called Kim. And I did something I hadn't done in years—I asked a woman for a date.

"Would you like to have dinner with me?"

There was a pause... then... quietly she asked, "Are you kidding?"

"No," I said. "Why wait until New Year's, how about this Friday?"

Her response was completely unfiltered and immediate as she loudly said, "Yes! I'd love to!"

I could feel that she really meant it. She was excited by the prospect of spending time with me! This was no small thing, no small thing at all! My excitement was hard to contain, too. I was both nervous and calm, anxious and ready, and I'd just hung up the phone! Hell, here I was, a grown man, feeling like a kid looking forward to his first date. It was, after all, my first real date in a long, long time.

Friday finally came. and we met at a small restaurant we picked randomly because it was halfway between our homes (turned out we lived about forty miles from each other). She pulled into the parking lot as I got out of my car, perfect timing. We both had red cars. "Hey, how about that?"

And we proceeded to have the most forgettable dinner of my life.

I don't remember what we ate or drank, or for that matter, where that restaurant was. I do know that I was completely taken by Kim. Our conversation flowed, apparently for hours, because this little strip center eatery closed up around us without my noticing. The owner, slightly embarrassed, finally and in a hushed tone, informed us that they were closed. Not wanting to end the evening, we met at a winery to continue talking, to keep getting to know more about each other. By now, I was completely at ease with her. I had watched her from a distance for some months, yet after just a couple of hours of one-on-one, straight-up, eye-to-eye honest and very fun talking, I trusted her, and told her the truth of my story. And she told me hers: she had four kids at home. Most women would have run when they heard my story, and most guys, I guess, would hightail it when they heard about the four kids, but we agreed to see each other again.

Truth be told, I wouldn't have cared if she had ten kids and twelve Billy goats; I really liked her. Rick was right. Kim is special. In fact, she is the most amazing person I've ever known. Since that first dinner, I've only wanted to be with her, and fortunately for me, she's felt the same.

The spinal surgeon brought in a vocal cord specialist to assist with the surgery. Fusing my third through sixth vertebrae required accessing my spine through my throat, therefore putting my vocal chords directly in harm's way. With the addition of this specialist, I was still only given a 50 percent chance of being able to sing again. Fifty percent. That was scary. Singing had brought me back from a dark, dark place, and to lose my ability to sing would be horrible. More than that, I had come to realize that it was my singing or my involvement with music that had been the positive force throughout my life. Whenever I had left music or the business of music out of my life professionally, I was never happy. Now, I no longer had the mental capacity to promote and produce shows, so singing was my only outlet and connection to the music, making the reality of losing it all the more frightening.

Two months after the surgery, I did a show at a club where I had played monthly for the last couple of years. It was rough, but I did it. The pain caused by that little slip on that summer afternoon, unfortunately, was not completely relieved by that major surgery. My ability to perform was impacted by not just the pain, but also by the restricted movements in my neck and by the pain medications. It took me days to recover from that show. Being determined or maybe stubborn is a better word, I booked another gig, and the same result. The recovery time for a two-hour gig was two or three days of painful bed rest. This pattern went on for months. Physical therapy and more and different meds didn't change things; my neck barely moved and still hurt like hell. The pattern was clear...

The accident that resulted in my having the spinal fusion surgery disrupted the carefully crafted plan I had developed for my "renewed" singing career. To perform five or six shows per week, let alone the dreams of overseas tours, was physically beyond me now. To sing locally, more as a hobbyist than as a pro, took some time to get used to, I gotta tell you. Yet, once I took an overview of my anything-but-ordinary life, I am thankful even for this. You see, it's the quality that counts. My life, at this point, is touched by astonishing quality at every turn. Great musicians accompany me when I sing, and when my phone rings, it often carries the voice of a friend I've had for forty years or more. My children, grown and successfully navigating their own lives, bring me a special kind of joy, and thanks to my son, I'm even a grandparent. Kim's children have welcomed me into the fold, and her brothers and parents treat me as family, too. So, after all of those years of chasing my dreams, of looking for success and acceptance, I have finally found those things. And the memories of having walked and worked and played with such giants as Frank Sinatra, Ray Charles, Luciano Pavarotti, and so many other geniuses, well, I'm just glad to have recaptured them, along with the other memories I've regained.

But best of all is Kim. She stands by me always, even when I forget the simplest things, time after time, and patiently helps me navigate my way through my unique world, which she has come to understand.

My life, so far, has been magical. Sure, I've had my share of wins and losses, huge swings from high to low, but what a life so far. Whenever I think of the people and places that I've been privileged to be touched by, I am eternally thankful. To think that I nearly lost all of the memories, both good and bad, is frightening. I realize that I still don't recall many things, and perhaps my recall may not be exact, but what a blessing to be able to draw on my experience.

I've done a lot so far, and if you asked me eight or ten years ago, I'd have said I was done—it was all over for me.

But not now, not even close. I've got to admit, it's different, but again, it's about quality now. I may not perform night after night, jumping from club to club, gig to gig, all in a blur of action and mediocre performances. Now, I may do a show three or four times per month, which allows me to concentrate more on the quality and the content of the show. I remember as a kid, my mother said that it was better to have one good suit than to have five cheap ones... well, the same applies to performing. I see so many club musicians and singers working so hard to get and keep gigs that they are too busy to maintain and improve the quality of their performance. I get it; it's a difficult balancing act, and often one that club owners and the audience don't require. I'm just happy to be off of that ever-spinning wheel. Now, I can concentrate on and deliver quality.

There are more benefits to being me, oh yeah, besides forgetting key things at important moments, like lyrics while singing to a full house and crying in public at things that make people stare at you. Oh, yeah, there are definitely more! One benefit is that I now feel successful. Even as a young man, I never equated success with money, not in the conventional sense. I chased the almighty dollar like most of us, realizing that needs must be met, but beyond that, I never gave money much thought. Maybe I should have planned better. No maybe about it! I should have, but I never had an education around money, and as a young man, it was just flowing, and I thought it would never stop. When it stopped, no matter how low things were, I had faith in myself that I'd turn it around, and I mostly did. But my point here is that money was not my driving force—passion was. Whenever I was excited about a project, a show, a concert or a series of them, a deal or a new idea, it seemed that the money would follow. Conversely, those "opportunities" that appealed to me only because of the financial potential, well, those deals seemed to most often come up short. No, my idea of success wasn't anchored in a bank balance, but by quality of life. The balance in my business "quality of life" account generally throughout my life was pretty damn good. I'm proud of the work I've done and the wonderful people I did it with. My past, when it comes to my personal relationships, well, those earlier choices led to the equivalent of emotional bankruptcy. This set up an imbalanced existence for many years: happy with work, not so much at home. Now, although nothing is ever perfect, I feel that success is finally in hand. With a more balanced budget both personally and professionally, for the first time in my life, I can say something many people may take for granted.

I can say that I'm happy.

Made in United States
North Haven, CT
03 June 2024

53257091R00157